ASSET FINANCE AND LEASING HANDBOOK

RICHARD GRANT
&
DAVID GENT

Woodhead-Faulkner
New York London Toronto Sydney Tokyo Singapore

Published by Woodhead-Faulkner (Publishers) Limited,
Simon & Schuster International Group,
Fitzwilliam House, 32 Trumpington Street,
Cambridge CB2 1QY, England

First published 1992

British Library Cataloguing in Publication Data
Grant, Richard
Asset finance and leasing handbook.
I. Title   II. Gent, David
658.15

ISBN 1-85941-780-8

Typeset by Goodfellow & Egan Ltd, Cambridge
Printed in Great Britain by BPCC Wheatons Ltd, Exeter

CONTENTS

---------------- † ----------------

PREFACE

This book provides an overview of the United Kingdom finance industry for the user wishing to compare leasing with other methods of short- or medium-term funding for the acquisition of plant and equipment, and for the financier wishing to increase, revise or update his or her knowledge of the industry. It will prove to be of particular value as background reading for those studying for recognised industry examinations in finance and banking practice.

The content will assume some limited, prior knowledge and has been written to provide an insight into the domestic areas of the UK asset finance industry. It is a general work and includes chapters on current product marketing methods, insurance-related packages and risk management, together with an examination of the current UK taxation implications and practices.

SSAP 21 accounting requirements for the various types of contract, together with an attempt to assess future Inland Revenue practices with regard to the Standard have been covered.

Subheadings have been used throughout in order to assist quick access to salient points, and a glossary of technical terms is contained in an Appendix. There are checklists of the information required to underwrite a credit transaction and to provide a basis for financial modelling to compare the cashflows generated by competing products, using discounted cashflow analysis.

The law is as at 1 August 1991, and Inland Revenue Statements of Practice are as at 1 August 1991

R. J. Grant

---------------- ⸶ ----------------

INTRODUCTION

The products

A businessperson wishing to acquire assets for use in his or her business is presented with a wide choice of ways in which the financing can be accommodated. Despite the apparent flexibility of the profiles, the choice will essentially be between the three categories of loan, hire purchase and leasing. The financial benefits alone may show there is little to choose between the competing forms of funding, when tax benefits available to the customer and financier are taken into account. However, the legal distinctions between these arrangements are fundamental, affecting the issues of ownership, security, title and balance sheet reporting.

Where the customer elects to acquire equipment by payment of rentals under a leasing arrangement, the financial institution purchasing and providing the asset will be regarded as the legal owner and the customer (or lessee) the bailee, or person in possession. Alternatively, should the customer elect to acquire the asset by means of some form of loan and secured by a charge over the equipment, the law will look upon the user as the owner, and the rights of the financier will be limited to those of mortgagee. Hire purchase is in many respects a hybrid lying between these disciplines.

The marketplace

The continued acceptability and resultant growth of leasing products in the United Kingdom, has surpassed the expectations of many financial commentators. Many had predicted a decline in the use of facilities during the years following the Chancellor's announcement, in his Budget speech of 13 March 1984, that it was his intention to withdraw the 100 per cent first year capital allowances.

Indeed, figures reported by the Equipment Leasing Association suggest that traditional lease products now account for around 20 per cent of all capital expenditure in the United Kingdom, a leasing market valued in 1990 at approximately £9.4 billion. In 1991, the leased assets acquired amounted to some £10.3 billion, with association members owning virtually £43 billion worth of assets on lease. When contracts allowing for a purchase option are included, this figure increases to £49 billion worth of assets.

The growth of leasing products has encouraged the formation of a variety of lessor companies, some specialising in specific asset types, others offering their products through manufacturer-based schemes while the general lessor has been willing to consider a very wide range of assets for an even wider ranging customer profile.

Accounting and taxation considerations

There are often complications in leasing when the asset is considered to become a fixture to land, but these principles will nevertheless also apply to the other forms of financial arrangement.

The accounting treatment of the alternative financing methods will mainly ignore the legal differences since the adoption of SSAP 21. However, the taxation treatment will generally follow from accepted legal distinctions, although the computation of allowances will reflect the underlying accounting treatment in the published accounts.

It is the taxation consequences which will usually decide the method of funding chosen, although there may be circumstances in which the convenience of a particular product may out-weigh those other considerations. This might apply where the monetary value involved is modest in relation to the size of the business as a whole.

The parties to the contract will need to give careful consideration to the structure of the transaction, having due regard to taxation benefits and the effective useful life of the asset to the business.

The growth of leasing

Leasing has come a long way since its inception in the United Kingdom in 1960 when the first recorded contract was written for two injection moulding machines costing £18,000.

During the period between 1972 and 1984 when 100 per cent first year allowances were available, it was almost certainly the taxation implications of leasing which fuelled the expansion of the UK leasing industry. Since that era, the commercial attraction of leasing products in terms of security and flexibility has come to be generally recognised. These factors are likely to preserve leasing as one of the major methods of asset finance.

Recent years have seen a commitment on behalf of the clearing banks to apportion funds and tax shelter specifically to their leasing activity. As competition has increased, so the basis of funding has become more sophisticated in the attempt to protect margins, while holding the pricing structure at acceptable market rates.

Summary

Within this work we will consider these factors against the economic environment in the United Kingdom. Competition, increasing customer awareness and the reduction in capital allowances have all impacted on the profitability of the financial institutions, resulting in significant changes in the methods of marketing employed in winning and promoting new business.

It is in this area that we will start to consider the activity of the UK asset finance market of the 1990s.

CHAPTER 1

PRODUCT MARKETING

Introduction

The asset finance industry of the 1990s has evolved over the centuries. Analysis of the financing methods used as long ago as the Norman invasion of 1066 suggests that William the Conqueror probably rented most of his ships.

Leasing in its present form was first introduced into the United Kingdom from the United States in 1960. There is nothing new in the concept of borrowing and lending money, nor in the hiring of assets. It is the general acceptance by our present society, that borrowing for legitimate business purposes is acceptable, which has become one of the major factors in fuelling the growth which has taken place during the second half of the 1980s.

Financing can generally be divided into tax-based and non-tax-based, the latter representing all forms of leasing and enjoying a near 20 per cent share of the market. Clearing banks no longer enjoy their privileged position of being the first line of resort to satisfy the customer's needs. Tax incentives remain, although eroded by government fiscal policy over the years, and careful analysis of a project's future cashflows will be required to ascertain the right product and therefore the most appropriate source of financing.

The UK market is believed to support more than 150 competing lending institutions in the asset finance market. As a consequence, financiers have had to become far more proactive, each suggesting that they will respond to their customers' needs more professionally and with greater speed than the next. Even the role of the local bank manager has changed over recent years. The banks now employ highly trained specialists willing to visit customers at their premises, a significant move away from the concept of the general practitioner who, being mainly office based, dealt with all areas of the bank's business.

Recent developments

The banks and finance companies have come under attack from the building societies for their personal lending business. To compete with building societies, which are now able to offer many of the facilities required by their retail account customers, the clearing banks have had to introduce cheque book accounts which bear interest on cleared credit balances. This has impacted upon the clearing banker's source of 'cheap money', eroding margins, resulting in the need to become even more aware of the cost base and to search for new areas of potential profit. No longer can the clearing banker rely upon customers' funds on current account to supply the proportion of the short-term funding requirement, without payment of interest, that it once did. In future the clearing banker will need to reward customers with interest on their outstanding credit balances.

The United Kingdom has been 'part' of Europe for some time. Treaties signed in 1951, 1957 and 1972, and the Act of 1987, have reinforced European commitment to the establishment of the single, unified market. It is the intention, at least of the European Community (EC) at large, to instil the progressive realisation of an economic and monetary union. This culture has increased competition for the traditional sources of finance from new entrants to the marketplace, resulting in many of the attitudes which are seen today.

There has been some recent press comment criticising the clearing banks for their pricing structure. While it will always be possible to pick upon individual cases where the borrower has a grievance, due account should be taken of the risks and rewards to the financier who is placed in the position of supporting a new venture business when forecasts go astray. After all, if it were that easy to establish and grow a business of one's own, there would be no one willing to be in the employ of the lending institutions!

However, there is perhaps one general criticism of the lending institutions. This relates to the methods adopted to encourage the businessperson to enter into credit arrangements, without the financier necessarily being fully aware of all the financial circumstances of the target customer. All too often, business is written on the scantiest of historic financial information, in a bid to offer the customer the fastest service to accommodate the purchase. How financiers target and then market their customers will now be considered.

Market focus

There are two principal approaches which depend upon the complexion of the financier. These approaches are either industry based or economically based.

The industry-based approach

The smaller financier, or indeed the subsidiary of the larger organisation, will often focus attention on a specific market sector in which the personnel will have developed a specific expertise. Good examples are the farming or the printing industries, where the financier's staff will not only have personal experience of the market but also contacts will be built to assist in assessing each proposal and the anticipated depreciation rate of the assets for which finance is sought by the customer. This knowledge will be applied to assist the customer to acquire the funding for the asset in a manner which is prudent in the light of its anticipated working life in the customer's hands.

Advertising is mainly focused towards specific trade press and supplemented by attendance at a variety of trade shows. In this way the advertising budget can be limited, aiming specifically at the desired market.

Some financiers will attempt to build relationships with suppliers or manufacturers in order to encourage a symbiotic sales-aid type of relationship, which will assist the supplier to overcome his or her customer's price objections at the point of sale. Where the supplier is a national organisation, the financier will be expected to have the means to supply local support, both for new business development and for training the supplier's staff. It is commonplace, therefore, for the national supplier to insist that the financier has some form of branch network, or at the very least, local representation covering the whole of the financier's geographical area of operation.

The economically-based approach

The general financier, who does not limit transactions to specific market sectors, will still need to define a marketplace and train staff accordingly. In most cases this breed of financier will define a market according to the size of a prospect's business. In so doing the financier will establish some arbitrary limit, such as the amount of the issued share capital, the turnover, or the pre-tax profit, as a measure to define a marketing database.

There are various sources from which this information can be obtained. It is no longer necessary for the financier to search through many thousands of company records, as specialist agencies (such as Dun and Bradstreet) can provide company selections either in printed form or on computer disc.

The market definitions commonly used will be described as small ticket, middle ticket and large value, but the precise values used to separate the categories will vary widely between the financing institutions. Details of these definitions are as follows:

1. *Small ticket business*: Whatever the 'house limit' placed upon the perceived marketing potential, the small ticket customer will be viewed as the business which enters the market perhaps once to twice a year seeking finance for single, modestly priced fixed assets. Since earnings on a single transaction will be limited because of the size of the requirement, many financiers will attempt to deal with the transaction through the telephone. This can be to the customer's advantage, of course, since the time otherwise spent in lengthy financial meetings can be more profitably used in running the business, a fact which is particularly true for the entrepreneurial sole trader.

The clearing banker may be more agreeable to a meeting, but the customer will generally find that it is necessary to visit the bank, and on doing so will be confronted with information on a whole range of other products which the bank is able to provide. Useful maybe, but the role of a good local accountant should not be overlooked.

2. *Middle ticket business*: This is the category which many general financiers view as the most attractive. Again, value limits used to define the market will vary significantly, but the attraction of the successful, growing business will be there for all. Each lender will work hard at endeavouring to build a relationship for the future, hoping to be the one who is always considered before the competition gains a competitive edge.

Bank managers are usually willing to call by appointment at regular intervals to discuss the progress of the customer's business. A specific management team will often be assigned to the account, providing the customer with the benefit of having specific points of contact for his or her various requirements and building a relationship which will help to deter competition.

The middle ticket customer is attractive to financiers and will probably receive many telephone calls offering to discuss an entire range of financial products.

3. *Large value transactions*: The market generally regards large value deals as those representing investments of at least £10 million and by their nature they will almost always require some definitive expertise on behalf of the

financier, if only at the least to be able to raise the required funding at the right profile and at an acceptable price.

Clearing banks will often appoint a coordinator for large value prospects and customers alike, in order that all dialogues are fully recorded and information shared between relevant specialists. The large value customer will represent a variety of 'cross-selling' opportunities, and the bank may be willing to afford a fluctuating overdraft facility at near cost in order to create other income earning opportunities.

Fee income for transactions with large value customers is often significant, reflecting the amount of time and expertise employed by senior managers in the financier's employ who have structured the contract.

Databases

Any good salesperson will know the value of holding an accurate and up-to-date database of prospects and customers. Prospect cards and manual files are rapidly giving way to computer-based information, now that the costs of personal computers and local area networks are beginning to fall. Computerisation of the database provides the benefit of rapidly accessing a range of data, whether for marketing purposes or for providing the answer to a customer enquiry. Nevertheless, as anyone with a computer system will be aware, they do sometimes 'fall over', and the skill of the sales team will be paramount in providing customer care when this happens.

There is always the temptation to hold too much data and for too long. The former may fall within the realms of the Data Protection Act and care should always be taken in recording any personal information on a computer. In the latter case, nothing changes. Just as no one likes to remove information from any file, manual or elctronic, files become full and take up space. A regular updating process should be installed, and a review of the quality of information will be vital if the user is going to maintain a competitive edge.

A marketing database will generally hold all the information necessary to contact the prospect (or customer) quickly and effectively, mindful of recent past experiences. Computerisation should simply speed up this process. The type of detail held may well comprise the following:

- Business name,
- Trading style,
- Address,
- Post code,

- Contact name,
- Contact status,
- Telephone numbers,
- Nature of the business,
- Year established,
- Bank details,
- Number of employees,
- Issued share capital,
- Previous year's profit,
- Industry description,
- Detail of previous dealings,
- Date of last contact,
- Essence of previous discussion,
- Detail of existing contracts with the financier,
- When, if at all, audited accounts were received,
- Payment history,
- Salesperson's notes.

Analysis of the database

Where the data records have been computerised, it should be a relatively straightforward task to investigate which business types in which geographical locations purchase equipment and at what part of the year. Such analysis will cut down the amount of time spent on establishing contact with businesses which are not currently in the market for funds. When an approach is made, the prospect is more likely to be receptive because there will be an impending requirement. The same task can, of course, be carried out on a manual system, but this will inevitably take longer to achieve for the salesperson who is new and therefore has limited knowledge of the territory.

One of the most useful pieces of information associated with such an analysis is the SIC code (standard industry classification code) which defines a business according to its principal activity. For marketing purposes, the code would generally be recorded to two decimal places. By searching other criteria against the code, a whole range of information relating to the spending patterns of businesses within an industry should become apparent.

Marketing initiatives

To establish an initial contact, the financier has four basic options, which are advertising, mailing, telephoning and cold calling.

1. *Advertising*: While some advertising will be aimed directly at generating business, inviting the prospect to contact the advertiser for information, there is a growing trend to focus advertisements in order to increase customer awareness, and to support local sales initiatives. This is particularly true of the larger financiers who have, presumably, larger advertising budgets.

2. *Mailing*: For some years the mailshot has proved to be an attractive method of establishing direct contact with the decision maker. Laser printed, computer based print-out looks very professional. The result looks like a personally addressed letter. However, as the cost has fallen, such systems are becoming commonplace with the result that their impact is diminished, as the prospective purchaser grows more accustomed to a high volume of marketing correspondence of this type.

Mailshots will generally be brief, designed to get their message across before the prospect loses interest and consigns the letter to the bin. Sometimes mailshots are transmitted by facsimile, or by telex, in an attempt to stress a level of urgency about a limited offer.

3. *Telephoning*: Most targeted mailshots will be followed up by a telephone call. More general and therefore, larger mailshots may not. The objective of the caller will be to speak with the decision maker and to ascertain what, if any, capital expenditure may be planned during coming months, and if it is substantial to call to discuss the benefits of those of the caller's products which best suit the customer's needs.

Smaller deals will often be concluded through the telephone, and indeed regular business relationships can be established in this way although neither party have ever met.

4. *Cold calling*: Although a salesperson may call at a company's premises while at the location to gather information, the practice of cold calling on prospects is one which appears to be dying out. This is in part due to the high cost of employing salespeople, and also to the resistance of the prospect to enter into a financial dialogue without some degree of preparation.

Relationship lending

The most successful financiers develop relationships with their customers, often marking facilities forward to cater for a range of future requirements. There is more profit to be made out of a customer with several agreements, because the initial cost of establishing the relationship is then recouped from the income generated by a number of contracts.

Relationships are important to both sides, since the customer, who is well established with the providers of funding, is more likely to receive support if trading becomes difficult for a time. An understanding of each others' requirements will develop, and the time spent by the financier reporting to his or her credit committee will be reduced, thereby saving costs and improving the customer service.

The price

Financial institutions have awoken to the fact that they can charge for specific services carried out. This is justifiable as the customer benefits from a wealth of expertise and an investment in technology which the financier has to offer. However, if the customer is dissatisfied with the service which is being purchased, the customer will be free to seek alternative sources of funding.

From the institutions' view point, charging for services has become a necessary reality as increasing competition in the market has driven down margins. The financier needs to look for alternative sources of income beyond the return on the funds employed, in order to justify the margins negotiated to the shareholders.

Sales-aid relationships

Sales-aid in the 1990s looks set to increase its market share significantly. It is attractive to the manufacturer (or supplier) because it helps to overcome the customer's price objections and will normally result in a payment from the financier within a relatively short period.

It is also attractive to the financier since the supplier is employing the salesperson to negotiate the sale. This increases the number of customer calls made without a proportionate increase in the financier's cost. In return the financier will usually agree to provide training for the supplier's salesforce. It can be appealing for the customer since all the potentially loose ends relating to the purchase can be tied up at one time and in one meeting. As a result, the customer is then in a position of dealing with only one sales contact to conclude the transaction.

Social functions

The established customer or the prospect, who is receiving overtures from the financier, may well be invited to some form of sponsored event. This is in part a reward for loyalty, but the financier will use the occasion as an opportunity to demonstrate to prospective buyers that the financier has an edge over competitors as evidenced by the customer profile present.

Promotional occasions may be organised nationally, such as a golfing weekend, or locally, by sponsorship of a local sporting event. It will be a chance for the customer to meet the support staff together with some of the senior management from within the financier's organisation.

Corporate identity

The financier will want to have a unique identity, which, in the case of a group of companies will serve to link the common relationship in the eyes of the outside world. Some organisations may also publish a mission statement which defines the basis of the existence of the business to staff and outsiders alike.

There will generally be a standard typeface and method of laying out the written word, running into the style and format of standard documentation, stationery and all types of correspondence. Once established, the corporate style will rarely change dramatically, amendments being introduced gradually and with thought regarding their impact on the customer. To a financier, the documentation is a vital part of the product, and even minor changes can cause an adverse reaction from a customer who has become used to a specific format over the years.

Business gifts

There is now a very wide range of promotional gifts available, ranging from writing sets to umbrellas, all designed to keep the customer aware of the financier's existence. Desk diaries are still the most popular means of drawing the financier's activity to the customer's attention, since once in use they represent a daily reminder of the relationship.

Statement enclosures

Most statements of account will be accompanied by leaflets advertising other products from the financier and/or associates. This appears to be an effective way of cross-selling services which ultimately increases the potential profitability from the customer source.

Summary

The approach will vary depending upon the specialisation of the financier, but the ethos of accuracy and quality should be prominent in any marketing strategy. If it is, then it is likely that the conversion rate of prospect to customer will be sufficient to justify the cost of further campaigns.

Variety, blended with consistency will be an important issue in the approach to marketing. There will need to be constant attention to detail and a recognition that the customer, whether internal or external, is the vital ingredient for the success of the business.

Adequate control of marketing costs will also be a key area in the ability to price products at an acceptable level in the chosen markets. Much can be achieved by converting the existing customer to other products as the additional costs involved should be less than converting an entirely new customer. Customer care will be a most important ingredient for success in the generation of additional new business from existing customers.

CHAPTER 2

TAXATION AND ACCOUNTING DIFFERENCES BETWEEN THE PRODUCTS

Finance and operating leases

There are two fundamental categories of lease in the United Kingdom and all lease agreements will fit into one or the other.

Finance leases

A finance lease is a lease during the term of which the lessor will expect to recoup the full cost of acquisition of the asset together with a return, the lessor's financing charge, representing overhead recovery and profit. The lease will commonly be divided into the following three parts:

1. The basic lease period: during which the lessee pays rentals to the lessor for the use of the asset. At the end of this period, the lessor will usually expect to have recouped the initial capital outlay plus the financing charge.
2. An optional renewal period: in this secondary period the lessee may continue to lease the equipment at his or her discretion. The rentals during this extension will normally be very much lower than those charged in the basic term, often at a rate of 1–2 per cent of the original capital cost and payable annually in advance.
3. The residual value sharing: at the end of the leasing it is common practice for the lessee to be invited to dispose of the equipment on behalf of the lessor. The lessee will then be permitted to retain the bulk of the sale proceeds, either as a refund of rentals, or as a sales agency commission.

Operating leases

During an operating lease the lessee will pay rentals which represent the depreciation of the asset during the period of use, and the residual value remaining still to be recouped will be the lessor's responsibility. The lessor will rely either upon a further period of rental, or the disposal of the asset, to realise the full potential of the investment in the lease.

The concept of economic ownership

Effectively, economic ownership passes to the lessee under the terms of a finance lease. The lessee will generally be contractually liable for insurance, maintenance and even disposal of the asset, in a similar manner to the instance where the lessee actually owns it. The lessee is therefore seen to assume most of the risks and rewards appertaining to ownership.

Under an operating contract the lessee will simply pay rentals for the use of the asset while being permitted such use, and the lease contract will be for a period of less than the perceived full useful life of the asset. The responsibility for the residual value remaining in the asset at the end of the lease term will be the responsibility of the lessor.

The characteristics of the lease types

Neither company law nor fiscal legislation seek to distinguish between the categories of lease, but commercially the differences are well known. The principal characteristics of these contracts are listed below.

Finance lease

The lease term will usually cover the whole (or almost the whole) of the working life of the asset.

Upon settlement before the end of the term, there will usually be a provision for the lessee to pay the balance of the outstanding rentals less a discount to reflect early termination.

Maintenance, repair and insurance will be the lessee's responsibility.

Ownership risks of loss, mechanical breakdown and obsolescence, resulting in a poor residual value lie with the lessee.

Operating lease

The lessor will often offer the asset for rental several times during its useful life.

The lease period will either be of a relatively short duration, or the lessee will enjoy the right to break the contract at certain times and without penalty.

The lessor may include these items within the terms of the contract.

The risks of breakdown and obsolescence remain with the lessor.

Finance lease	*Operating lease*
The lessee will often control ordering, delivery and disposal.	The lessor will often supply the asset.
The larger share of the disposal proceeds will pass to the lessee either as a commission for disposal or as a refund of rentals.	The proceeds of disposal will be the exclusive right of the lessor.

Statement of Standard Accounting Practice

It is not only the total number and the amount of the rentals which will guide us to the type of lease which is being proposed. Close examination of the substance of the contract in question may cause us to reach a conclusion which is less obvious than the apparent form. As the expertise of the financial institutions in assessing anticipated residual values of a range of assets increases, increasingly complex transactions will evolve.

It is the debate over substance versus form which continues to occupy the minds of the accountancy professions, whose responsibility it is to report accurately on the state of affairs of a business. The Accounting Standards Committee published its Statement of Standard Accounting Practice on accounting for leases and hire purchase in August 1984. That statement (SSAP 21) defines a finance lease as a lease that transfers substantially all the risks and rewards of ownership to the lessee and an operating lease as any lease other than a finance lease.

While, for the purposes of this definition, it is to be assumed that a transfer of risks and rewards occurs if, at the start of the lease, the present value of the minimum lease payments (calculated by using the rate implicit in the lease) amounts to substantially all of the fair market value of the leased asset. 'Substantially all of the fair market value' has generally been taken to be 90 per cent or more of the price at which the asset would be exchanged in an arms length transaction, less any grants which may be available.

The minimum lease payments are defined as being the minimum rental payments over the remainder of the lease term. In arriving at the payments, charges for taxes (such as Value Added Tax) and services to be paid by the lessor will be excluded. Any sum which the lessee may have guaranteed in relation to the residual value of the asset at the end of the lease term will, however, be included.

In the case of the lessor, the minimum lease payments also include any residual amount guaranteed by the lessee, or, by a third party. It can be seen, therefore, that the classification of the lease for accounting purposes will not necessarily be the same for both the lessee and the lessor. An operating lease to the lessee may still be recorded as a finance lease to the lessor because of a residual value guarantee from a dealer.

It is most important that independent professional advice be sought prior to entry into a contract where such a question of doubt arises, and when, for balance sheet reporting, the classification of the lease may have a material impact.

A detailed account of the requirements of SSAP 21 is given in Chapter 14. As for the future, there is currently a debate regarding the need for a further SSAP to address these issues.

The tax treatment of contracts

The legal relationships created by finance and operating leases are comparable, but hire purchase is not. Hire purchase is defined simply as hiring with the option to purchase. In leasing this purchase option is specifically denied to the lessee, or indeed to any party connected with the lessee, at the outset, and the treatment for tax purposes reflects these basic differences.

A person who lets goods on hire purchase is generally regarded as dealing in them, whereas someone who leases them is treated as acquiring capital assets which he or she makes available for hire with a view to profit. The difference may at first sight seem to be subtle, but in essence the badge of trade comes about in the case of hire purchase because of the repetitive nature of transactions which ultimately result in the disposal of goods; a leasing transaction does not. The lessor is seen to hold assets for the purposes of generating a rental stream in the pursuit of profit.

Because hire purchase is viewed as the dealing in goods, it is the hirer and not the financier who will be able to claim and retain capital allowances for which the goods may qualify; provided of course that those goods are genuinely acquired for the purposes of the customer's qualifying business. As assets employed in a leasing transaction are regarded as being of a capital nature, it is the lessor who will be entitled to claim the capital allowances which are available.

It is appropriate to note that should a hire purchase contract be structured with a high residual value placed upon the asset, and at the end of the term a third party contracts to purchase (or repurchase) the asset, the right to capital allowances claimed by the customer may be forfeited. This is because the Revenue will query that an option to purchase by the customer was truly available.

Conditions in contracts

Finance leases and hire purchase contracts will often contain terms which at first sight appear similar to those of loan agreements. Provisions in hire purchase documents dealing with the calculation of finance charges, and interest charges on late payments, will often seem to be drafted in a similar manner to those of loan agreements. However, the fact that hire payments are calculated by reference to a given rate of interest does not mean that the corresponding element of the payment has the character of interest.

For a payment to amount to interest, two requirements need to be satisfied. First, there must be a sum of money by reference to which the payment said to be of interest is to be defined and, second, that sum of money must be due to the persons entitled to the interest (Chevron Petroleum (UK) Limited v. BP Petroleum Development [1981] STC 689).

In the case of hire purchase (or indeed finance leasing), the first point will be satisfied, since rentals (and charges) will be calculated by reference to the initial cost (the cash price or principal amount). However, the second point will not. This is because the cash price is not the amount owed; the customer's obligation being to make rental payments on predetermined dates and in a predetermined manner, even though there may be some acceleration of future rentals in the event of a default or early termination of the contract.

Summary

In summary, under a hire purchase contract it is the customer who will be entitled to the capital allowances available with reference to the asset. Interest charges will be deducted from profit in the accounting period in which they fall due and payable (provided of course that they have been paid on the due dates). An accruals basis will generally be applied.

Under a leasing contract, the customer (the lessee) will charge the rentals against income, or apportion depreciation and finance charge relating to the rentals on an accruals basis, leaving the lessor to claim his entitlement to any capital allowances which may be available.

In the case of a loan, the customer will charge interest against profit on an accruals basis and claim the capital allowance entitlement in respect of the asset.

CHAPTER 3

†

THE TAX POSITION OF THE LESSOR AND THE LESSEE

THE LESSOR'S TAX POSITION

The trade of leasing

The lessor will need to become established as carrying on the trade of leasing in order to be certain of the availability of capital allowances. Should the lessor fail to do this, then there is a danger of being regarded as dealing in the equipment in question. Trading must be seen to be active. Should the activity be seen only as acquiring assets for the generation of sources of income, with nothing to be done by the owner in order to receive and enjoy the benefit of a rental stream, the characteristics will usually be regarded as those of an investment rather than those of a trade.

Operating lease companies, such as in plant hire or vehicle contract hire, are likely to have less difficulty in establishing the trading concept because they will be actively involved in maintaining and servicing their vehicle fleets. Finance lessors may have more difficulty, since the responsibilities with regard to maintenance, servicing and insurance generally pass to the lessee. In practice, however, provided the lessor has structured the business in anticipation of regular flows of new business, the lessor will not fail to be regarded as trading.

Capital allowances

Historically, one of the chief reasons for the growth in leasing activity was the availability of capital allowances. From 1972 to 1984, the owner of most types of equipment employed in a business was able to claim 100 per cent of the cost of equipment as a capital allowance at the end of the year of acquisition. The period 1984 to 1986 saw the value of this allowance scaled down year on year to 75 per cent, then to 50 per cent and finally to the present writing down basis at a rate of 25 per cent per annum.

Despite mainstream corporation tax coming down from 52 per cent to 35 per cent, this reduction in the value of capital allowances potentially caused cashflow problems to industrial concerns which were accustomed to acquiring assets for relatively short-term projects. They would from then on be in the position of writing off their plant over periods in excess of ten years, as a result of the new fiscal policy.

The short life asset election

This was recognised by government and the Finance Act of 1985 contained provisions in its section 57, to allow a business to elect to de-pool those assets which were considered to be short life in nature. This allowed for the balance of the tax written down value to be claimed as a balancing allowance, provided that disposal took place on or before the fourth anniversary of the end of the year of acquisition (deemed to be the year in which the purchase price was due and payable in full, or in which the first progress payment fell due, if sooner).

The effect on lease rentals

This ability to balance allowances within a limited time scale has inevitably proved of importance to the lessor in evaluating rental streams. If it is assumed that the balance of expenditure (or tax written down value) can be claimed at the end of the lease term when the asset subject to the lease is sold, the rentals during that lease term are likely to be considerably reduced. However, if at the point of expected disposal the lessee, under the terms of a finance lease, elects to continue into a secondary rental period, the benefit accruing to the lessor to accelerate the allowance claim will be lost. There will then be a need to charge additional rentals to fund the cashflow extension which will result.

The two most common methods employed will be either to enhance the secondary rental price, or to charge a single additional rental. The objective in either case will be to recoup the interest cost suffered by the lessor and therefore to maintain the post-tax return.

In smaller value contracts, it is often the case that the calculation will be imprecise, taking little or no account of cost of funds current at the time of the election to extend the lease. Many lessees are content to accept the benefits they perceive in the form of cheaper rentals in the early years and relying on inflation to reduce any potential cashflow disadvantage caused by the increased secondary rentals.

Example 3.1 De-pooling
A company purchases a lathe and a printing machine. They are brought into use on 31 March 1990, the company's year-end. Three years later, disposal of the printing machine takes place, but the lathe is retained. The sale of the printing equipment is successful and the sale proceeds are £10,000.

Company's year-end	Printing machine (£)	Lathe (£)	Allowances (£)
31.3.90 (Year of acquisition)			
Additions	25,000	25,000	
Writing down allowance (WDA) at 25%	(6,250)	(6,250)	12,500
Qualifying expenditure carried forward	18,750	18,750	
31.3.91 (End of first year)			
WDA at 25%	(4,687)	(4,687)	9,374
Qualifying expenditure carried forward	14,063	14,063	
31.3.92 (End of second year)			
WDA at 25%	(3,516)	(3,516)	7,032
Qualifying expenditure carried forward	10,547	10,547	
31.3.93 (End of third year)			
Sale of printing machine:	(10,000)		
Balancing allowance	(547)		547
WDA at 25%		(2,637)	2,637
Total allowances in year			3,184
Qualifying expenditure carried forward		7,910	

31.3.94 The fourth anniversary of end of year of acquisition. (If disposal has not occurred by this date the tax written down value must be transferred to the general pool of capital expenditure.)

WDA at 25%		(1,977)	1,977
Qualifying expenditure transferred to general pool		5,933	

Within the general pool the asset value will continue to be written down at a rate of 25 per cent per annum. For the lessor, who has evaluated a lease to reflect the benefit of the short life asset election, there will need to be some provision within the lease documentation to compensate for the time which it will take to write-off the asset in the extension period.

Generally, in many but the smallest transactions, there will be a clause in the lease providing for an additional rental to become payable based upon the lessor's position if sale proceeds fail to equal the tax written down value at the time of disposal. This, where it appears, should always be quantified by the lessee, as the potential liability could materially affect the rate implicit in the lease.

Tax on trading income of the lessor

In the view of the Inland Revenue, the trading income of the lessor will normally be the whole of the rental due under the terms of the lease agreement in the relevant accounting period on an accruals basis. It is of note that, for the purposes of producing annual accounts, the company will often adopt a different basis to arrive at the profit.

Methods which are more complex than those for hire purchase transactions have had to be adopted in order to take account of the availability of capital allowances. These methods reflect the timing of all cashflows, including the possible availability of grants, capital allowances and rental payments. SSAP 21 is regarded as the standard to be used as far as lessors are concerned, and this will be discussed in detail in Chapter 14.

The taxation of income

It is a basic principle of income taxation that the treatment of receipts for tax purposes depends on whether they are, as a matter of law, of an income nature, rather than in accounting terms where they may be regarded as a return on capital invested, or the recovery of capital expenditure already incurred.

A flow of periodically recurring rentals over a period of time which have been calculated by some stipulated legal criteria will be regarded as comprising receipts purely of an income nature. As the cost of the leased asset is capital expenditure of the lessor, the apportionment of rentals, into recovery of that capital expenditure and finance charge, would effectively bring about a deduction from income of some part of that capital expenditure which is outside the scope of the capital allowances structure. This is why the whole of the rental receipt (excluding VAT) will be brought into the income computation for tax purposes.

This is at variance with the hire purchase company, where only the proportion of the rental receipts relating to the finance charge element of the total hire purchase price is brought into the computation. Because hire purchase financiers are regarded as trading in the goods, the cost of the goods on hire purchase should be deducted as a trading expense, whereupon the rental receipts would then become liable to taxation in full. Hire purchase accounting methods will usually short cut the process by the calculation of the finance charge element in the rental receipts.

In leasing the whole of the rental received will be offset by deduction of trading expenses and capital allowances in order to arrive at the taxable trading profit of the lessor. Rental payments will ordinarily be made on a normal accruals basis in the case of a trading lessor. This means that each rental is treated as accruing in the rental period to which it refers under the lease terms. It may be necessary to refer to the wording of the lease where rentals fall payable before the start of the period to which they are attributable in the lease (e.g. progress payment rentals), and where there are balloon rentals, in order to seek clarification as to the manner in which these should be treated.

Trading expenses

These expenses will fall into one of the accepted management accounting definitions of fixed, variable, semi-fixed or semi-variable. Fixed costs will include expenses such as office rent, rates and most basic salaries. They are costs which do not vary with the activity of the business. Variable costs will include vehicle operating expenses such as fuel, repairs and maintenance, as these will be activity related.

Provided all of these costs have been legitimately incurred in the pursuit of profit, they will be permitted as deductions from income in arriving at trading profit subject to taxation. Where an operating lease lessor is responsible for maintenance, repair and insurance these related costs will also be allowed as an expense against profit, provided that that expense is of a revenue nature (Law Shipping Co Limited v. IRC 12 STC 621).

Capital or revenue expenses

It will be important to recognise those costs relating to the provision of the asset which are capital in nature and those expenses incurred in providing the lease which will be of a revenue nature. This area can become very involved because the provision of the asset and the inception of the lease often appear as one commercial transaction.

Interest on the funds borrowed to acquire the leased equipment will usually represent a major expense. In the case of a corporate lessor, deduction of interest payable will be permitted, provided the interest is payable in the United Kingdom and the advance is made by a bank carrying on a bona fide business in the United Kingdom. However, that interest must be incurred wholly and exclusively in the course of trade – even yearly interest will be treated as an expense rather than a charge on income (Wilcock *v.* Frigate Investments Limited [1982] STC 198).

The period of the advance need not precisely match the period of the lease, and interest on borrowing of less than twelve months will qualify as an expense provided all relevant conditions are satisfied. Yearly interest on borrowing from other than a bank is generally treated as deductible from total profits as a charge on income, provided that it does not represent a distribution. This is significant because charges on income may not be carried back against total profits of the previous accounting period. In the case of an individual lessor, interest on borrowings used to finance the acquisition of equipment will be allowed as an expense, provided that it is wholly and exclusively incurred for trading purposes.

Bad debt relief

Bad debt relief may only be obtained against specific (named) bad debts proven to be bad or to the extent that they may reasonably be estimated to be bad. Hire purchase financiers are allowed a concession to deduct a reasonable general provision for bad debt where they are operating purely in the consumer field, and this concession may be available to the consumer-related operating lease lessor.

Other issues

There are other complex issues which can arise as a result of capital taxes resulting from the disposal of all or part of a leasing portfolio but these are considered to be outside the scope of this study.

THE LESSEE'S TAX POSITION

Introduction

The rentals paid, exclusive of VAT, will usually be allowable as a tax deductible expense where the lessee carries on a trade and the equipment subject to the lease is used for the purposes of that trade. This is a major difference when compared with hire purchase and reflects the nature of the transaction which is the payment for use of the asset for a period rather than the payment for ultimate ownership. The exception will be rental payments which are made in respect of private motor cars and the tax treatment will be expressly considered below.

The importance of lease structure

It is the principle of payment for use rather than ownership which means that disposal of the asset at the end of the term must be to a third party who is independent of the leasing transaction. A disposal to a connected party will potentially result in a loss of the tax benefits available to the lessor, and this will impact on the profitability of the transaction, as the lease evaluation will have taken such benefits into account.

This point will be significant in deciding on the rentals to be charged during a secondary or renewal period, since it will be important for the lessor to be seen to continue to charge a commercial rate, in order that there can be no suggestion that title to the asset has been passed to the lessee. Commercial practice currently shows that renewal period rentals will be charged at a peppercorn annual rental varying between 0.5 per cent and 5 per cent of original cost, the first of such rentals falling due and payable immediately following the end of the primary term of the lease.

Non-business use

Conversely, should the equipment only be used in part for business purposes, part of the rental payment will be disallowed for taxation purposes. Strictly speaking, as current legislation requires an asset to be used wholly and exclusively for business purposes, this should be considered to be a concession by the Revenue.

Private motor cars

Rental payments in respect of private motor vehicles are subject to a restriction of the amount of rental which may be claimed against tax. To the extent that the cost when new exceeds £8,000, the proportion of the rental relating to the cost in excess of £8,000 will be reduced by the formula:

$$\frac{£8,000 + (\text{actual cost when new} - £8,000)}{2}$$

In other words, only half of the rental payment relating to the cost in excess of £8,000 will be allowable. Example 3.2 will clarify this point.

Example 3.2 Car leasing
Assuming the cost of a car when new is £10,000, the proportion of the rental which may be deducted for tax purposes is:

$$\frac{£8,000 + (£10,000 - £8,000)}{2}$$

Therefore the percentage will be:

$$\frac{£9,000}{£10,000} \times 100\% = 90\%.$$

Therefore, 90 per cent of the rentals may be deducted.

Sharing of sale proceeds

In many cases the lessee will receive a payment by the lessor upon the disposal of the leased asset. Commonly, this payment will represent a figure of 90–99 per cent of the sale proceeds. This will be achieved by either appointing the lessee as the agent of the lessor to dispose of the equipment for the lessor and specifying a sales agency commission or, more commonly, by the lessor permitting a rental rebate. Any rebate of rentals will be charged to taxation in the year of receipt, to the extent that the rentals paid during the period of the lease were permitted as a deduction in computing taxable profits.

The lessor will generally prefer the lessee to dispose of the asset because this will save on the lessor's administration costs. It is also an incentive for the lessee to maintain and service the asset, because a larger sum will be obtained on the sale of the asset.

Revenue Statement of Practice for finance lease rental payments

On 11 April 1991 the Inland Revenue issued a Statement of Practice (SOP) regarding the tax treatment of finance lease rentals paid by lessees. This confirmed the Revenue's desire to address some leasing structures where the lessee's deductions were increased due to artificial front-loading of rentals. This decision seems to have been made because the Revenue felt that the discretion allowed to lessors in the way in which they account for lease rentals received, and the absence of liaison between local Inspectors of Taxes for each party to the transaction, was such that front-loading would not always be matched between the tax computation of the lessee and the lessor.

The Revenue's SOP defines the lessee as either a company covered by SSAP 21 or as an unincorporated business. Both categories will have to claim deduction of lease rentals paid on some sort of accruals basis over the life of the leased asset. For the SSAP 21 companies, it is assumed that they will make limited adjustments to the pattern of financing charges and depreciation of the leased asset which the SSAP requires in the profit and loss account. For the unincorporated businesses in section A of the SOP, the tax treatment prescribed does not cross refer to the accounting standard, although it is in part based upon the SSAP methodology. Rentals 'should be allocated to periods of account for which the asset is leased under the accruals concept'. Where there is a provision for a secondary period 'regard should be had not only to the primary period but also to the economic life of the asset and its likely period of use by the lessee'.

In the case of the incorporated bodies, there is no direct reference to 'economic life' nor to the secondary period of the lease in the paragraphs of the SOP which deal with the taxation treatment. However, the SOP does draw attention to SSAP 21 requirements relating to 'expected useful life in the hands of the lessee'.

For both categories of lessee, the Revenue accepts that in tax law the rentals are revenue in nature. For the SSAP 21 companies, adjustments may be made to tax computations on the basis of a notional split between depreciation and financing charges, in a comparable way to the accounting standard.

Where the lessee accounts in accordance with the Standard and applies normal commercially-based depreciation, the Revenue will accept the combined depreciation and the financing charge as deductible rentals in each year. Where normal commercial depreciation is not applied, the Revenue will allow 'such part of the rentals for the period as represents the properly calculated proportion of the capital repayment element, which should be allocated to the period in accordance with the accruals concept'.

The SOP will apply to leases written after the date of its publication and is not retrospective. The tax position of lessors remains unchanged. The accounting principles contained within SSAP 21 will be considered in detail in Chapter 14.

CHAPTER 4

—— ⸸ ——

HIRE PURCHASE: THE TAX
POSITION OF THE PARTIES

THE OWNER'S TAX POSITION

Introduction

The method of treatment of hire purchase instalments in the hands of the owner will be dependent upon the business of the hire purchase financier being of a financing nature. In the normal situation, wherein the owner of the equipment subject to hire purchase is taken to be trading in that equipment, all receipts will be trading receipts. A trade of hire purchase has been recognised by the courts as not being an ordinary trade; because of the nature of the contract the trade has something of a hybrid character.

In strict legal terms, the receipts by a hire purchase company will comprise, initially, a consideration for the use of the equipment during the period of hire and, subsequently, the price of the purchase option. Finally, of course, the receipts will include the cost of the goods themselves. However, in their approach to the taxation of receipts, the Inland Revenue look to the fact that the goods are made available on extended payment terms with a charge for credit being applied.

The finance company v. the dealer

A finance company will differ from a retail trader who disposes of some stock by credit sale or hire purchase while the remainder is sold for cash, in so far as the cost of the goods to the finance company will be the usual retail selling price.

The profit of the finance company will rely exclusively upon the finance charge element of the hire purchase contract, while the dealer's profit will generally arise from two areas. The first of these will occur from the difference between the cost of the asset to the dealer and the selling price, and the second will be the charge for finance. It is the finance company therefore which more closely resembles the leasing company engaged in finance leasing.

Accounting for profit over the life of the agreement

Since all receipts of the finance company will generally be treated as being revenue in nature, the key to taxation treatment of those receipts will be the manner in which profit is allocated to various accounting periods, which span the life of the agreement.

The Revenue will generally be prepared to follow the finance company's own accounting basis of profit recognition, provided that the methods are employed consistently year on year and that they are reasonable in relation to the overall potential liability to taxation. This treatment will generally follow from the nature of the hire purchase company's business, which is essentially the provision of deferred payment terms for the sale of goods rather than the hiring and selling of goods at a profit. At the point of sale itself, no profit actually arises and a charge analogous to interest is applied, although as a matter of law this charge does not constitute interest.

As with loan interest, the finance charges are deemed to be earned over the life of the agreement and indeed the principal methods of apportioning those charges will produce cashflows similar to those arising from loan agreements.

The revenue from the hire purchase contracts of a finance company will consist of the following:

unearned charges brought forward at the beginning of the period of + the full amount of the charges accruing during the accounting account   period,

less, any unearned charges at the end of the period carried forward to the next period. These unearned charges will arise when the periods covered by the rental payments and the accounting period dates overlap. Option to purchase fees arising during the period will also be included in the income calculation.

Income allocation after SSAP 21

There is no statutory requirement regarding the methods of accounting for receipts, except for the fact that the company's audited accounts should show a true and fair view of the state of affairs of the business at the point when they are drawn up. SSAP 21 states that those hire purchase contracts which are of a financing nature should be accounted for on a basis similar to that for the finance lease.

Allocation of gross earnings between the respective accounting periods, so as to give a constant periodic rate of return on the finance company's net investment, will in most cases be a suitable approximation to an allocation based upon the net cash investment required in respect of finance leases. The net investment will be the gross investment (being the aggregate of the minimum hire purchase payments and any unguaranteed residual value accruing to the finance company), less gross earnings allocated to future periods. This is because the finance company's net investment will often be equal to, or virtually equal to, its net cash investment, because capital allowances will accrue to the hirer and not to the finance company.

As a result, finance companies normally account for their profits in respect of their hire purchase business in a way that does not reflect the effects of taxation. There are two principal methods which are the rule of 78 method, and the actuarial method before tax.

The rule of 78 method

Here the finance charges are reckoned to arise in relation to the amount of the outstanding capital. For instance, if a transaction is for a period of twelve months, with rentals payable by twelve equal instalments, there are twelve rentals still outstanding during the first month, eleven during the second, ten during the third month and so on until on the twelfth month only one rental remains to be paid. Each rental is considered to contain units of finance charge. There are twelve units of finance charge outstanding during the first month, eleven during the second, ten during the third month and so on until only one unit of finance charge remains in the twelfth month. This method attempts to reconcile the amount of finance charge in each payment with the amount of capital outstanding so that it is largest when the capital outstanding is at its highest and reduces throughout the term of the contract.

The sum of these units of finance charge in the twelve month example is 78 and therefore there are 12/78ths of the finance charge earned during month one, 11/78ths of the finance charge during month two, etc.

The method takes no account of the costs of establishing the contract to the finance company nor the failure to recoup those costs in the event of early settlement of the contract by the hirer.

The formula to express the component of finance charge during any period is as follows:

$$\frac{n(n + 1)}{2}$$

where n = the number of periods (months) in the contract.
The method is often referred to as the 'sum of digits' method.

The actuarial method before tax

Here finance charges are calculated on a strict reducing balance basis and the proportion of the charge decreases in each instalment as rentals are paid. As a result, the ratio of finance charge to principle outstanding is more accurately maintained than with the rule of 78.

The effect of applying this actuarial method is to produce a constant rate of return on the finance company's net investment (that is, broadly the amount of the cost price of the equipment for the time being outstanding). However, this method also fails to reflect the cost of establishing the contract, but some adjustment may be made to reflect the once and for all nature of the setting up costs by treating an amount equal to that initial expense as earned income at the start of the agreement.

The alternative methods of income allocation

While one or other of the above methods is most likely to be applied by the major finance company, alternatives and amendments will not be uncommon. SSAP 21 gives guidance notes in this respect, provided that such adoption achieves a reasonable approximation to profit recognition on the basis of a constant periodic rate of return.

Other methods used previously include the equal instalments method and the direct percentage method, although it is unlikely that either will find great favour while the emphasis placed upon other accounting methods exists under SSAP 21. For historical value a brief summary of these methods has been included.

The equal instalments method

Here the finance charge is regarded as accruing unevenly over the full term of the agreement in such a way that each rental comprises an equal and consistent element of both interest and capital repayment. In any particular agreement there is the danger of distortion in the rate of return occurring, as no attempt is made to reflect the charges in relation to the reducing outstanding capital balance.

This method has not proved to be popular with the finance companies and has been limited principally to dealers who offer hire purchase on their own account at the point of sale. It is appropriate to suggest that this method (which is also referred to as the straight line method) should be relevant to hire purchase transactions, which, not being of a financing nature, are more analogous to operating lease contracts. This application may be extended where the hirer has the option to purchase at market value of the asset at the time of the option, as distinct from financing transactions where the option fee will be of a nominal sum.

Finance companies themselves rarely engage in this type of transaction, but where they do, the Revenue will need to satisfy itself as to the precise nature of the transaction before deciding upon the reasonableness or otherwise of the accounting treatment.

The direct percentage method

The second and less common method is rather more complicated and involves the need to calculate the unearned finance charges, at the end of any accounting period, as a percentage of the total repayable under the terms of the agreement concerned.

In view of the nature of the method, the Revenue will need to be satisfied that the basis used to determine the percentage is a reasonable one before agreeing tax computations based upon this method of arriving at taxable profit. As with any matter in UK law, it is what is reasonable (and consistent) that will occupy the Revenue. Whichever method is adopted, the profit thereby calculated should be a prudent measure of the business's trading performance during each accounting period.

Grouping accounts

While the assumption has been made that the profit on single agreements is to be computed, it is frequently the case that finance companies will group agreements for accounting purposes into appropriate categories because of large volumes of business. Where this is done, reference will be made to the months in which they were incepted, the period of the agreement and the rate of finance charge applied. The appropriate method of profit assessment will then be applied. Accounts drawn up in this way will generally be acceptable to the Revenue for taxation purposes.

The owner's deductions in computing taxable profits

What is and what is not permitted as a deduction from profit will usually be decided by whether the owner is trading as a finance company, or as a trader in the goods offering point of sale finance as an aid to sales. The two principal categories relating to deductions will be trading expenses and provision for bad debts.

Trading expenses

In this category, items included will be:

- Interest,
- Dealer's commission,
- Cost of documentation,
- Legal costs relating to agreements,
- Collection costs,

all of which are specific to individual transactions or types of transactions. In addition, the variable and fixed costs of the business, including items such as light and heat, salaries and wages, vehicle operating costs etc. will be allowable as expenses and therefore will be deductible in arriving at the trading profit of the business.

Rebates allowed to hirers who settle their agreements early will also be permitted, and these will normally be taken into account at the point of arriving at the finance charges which have been earned.

Bad debt provisions

Bad debts will fall into either specific bad debts or a general reserve for bad debts, the latter usually being calculated on a formula basis.

When a hirer falls into default and the financier executes the right to terminate the agreement and to repossess the asset, the finance company will claim a specific deduction for the loss which has been suffered against that named debtor. The loss will be computed by reference to the balance of the rentals outstanding at the time of the termination by the finance company, less the unearned charges at the date of termination and the value of the asset which was repossessed. In the case of doubtful debts, the finance company will only be allowed to claim a deduction of a proportion of the potential loss after having due regard to the chances of recovery.

The agreement to allow the deduction of a bad debt reserve is contrary to

Inland Revenue custom in other industries, and it is incumbent upon the finance company to justify the reasonableness of the deduction which is claimed. Normally the general reserve will be calculated as a percentage of the balances outstanding, broken down into categories which reflect period, the nature of the asset, the source of the business, etc. and will only be accepted by the Revenue if that analysis reflects previous trading experience and the current economic climate.

The case of a dealer selling hire purchase

Where hire purchase is offered as an aid to sales on the dealer's own account and as an alternative to outright purchase, the calculation will be more complicated. This is because the dealer's profit arises from more than one source, unlike the finance company whose profit arises out of the finance charge element of the rental stream.

A dealer who enters into a hire purchase contract with the customer will first generate profit on the cash price of the goods sold, less a deduction reflecting the selling costs to the dealer (including the initial cost of the goods to the dealer). The dealer's second potential profit centre will be the finance charges themselves and any of the methods of accounting for these charges referred to above may be used.

Either the cash profit will be brought into account at the start of the agreement, or it may be spread over the life of the agreement. Where the latter option is selected, the cash profit will generally be spread equally over the period of the agreement, and the finance charges will then usually be apportioned using the equal instalment, or straight line, method. The reasonableness and consistency of the practice of the accounting method will decide its acceptability to the Revenue in most circumstances.

Alternatively, the dealer may ask for the calculation of profit to be based on the method agreed by the Hire Purchase Trade Association and the Inland Revenue back in 1928. Under this method (the HPTA method), the dealer will compute the closing figure for stock of goods out on hire purchase by first calculating the average rate of gross profit on all the hire purchase transactions conducted during the accounting period, and then reducing the outstanding hire purchase instalments at the year-end by the average rate of profit calculated in this way. The resulting trading profit will then consist of the aggregate of instalments received during the year, plus the amount by which the closing stock figure obtained in this way exceeds that of the opening stock.

Where this method is adopted, no general bad debts reserve will be deductible, although specific (named) debts will still be permitted. The method is concessionary and requires the dealer's books of account to be maintained in this fashion consistently year on year.

Funding by block discounting

Where a dealer has elected to fund the book of hire purchase debtors by way of a block discounting arrangement, the price payable to the dealer is brought into account at the date of the sale. This is despite the fact that the discounter will no doubt hold back a proportion of the value of the debts thereby sold by way of security against potential non-payment by customers of the dealer. Any additional proceeds subsequently received will be brought into account at the date they are received.

Contingencies in respect of guarantees

A dealer will often have a contingent liability to the customer in respect of a product guarantee or a warranty, despite the fact that the hire purchase transaction has been written with a finance company introduced by the dealer. Any provision made in the accounts in respect of such matters will generally be added back for the purposes of assessing taxation of profit, but the Revenue may allow a deduction, by concession, where any bad debt arises as a result of such guarantee or warranty.

The important point here is that no deduction may be permitted for a liability while it is considered to be merely contingent.

THE HIRER'S TAX POSITION

Introduction

The hirer is allowed both to hire the equipment for a predefined period and, at the end of the term, to purchase it from the owner. The hirer will therefore allocate the payments made between the amount which relates to the hire itself and an amount which relates to the purchase option. A trading company using the asset for trading purposes will treat the hire payments as a trading expense deducted from income; an investment company will regard such payments as a management expense. The payment in respect of the option to purchase the equipment at the end of the period will be treated as capital expenditure and will not therefore be deductible in the trading profit computation.

Inland Revenue practice

The practice of the Inland Revenue is to treat the cash price as representing the element of capital expenditure and the finance charges as the revenue expenditure. That is to say the finance company's profit is effectively the hirer's revenue expense.

The exception to this will be where the purchase option is to be at market value of the asset. When this is the case, no part of the hire purchase instalment should be treated as contributing to the option to purchase and as a result the rental payments will be deducted in full as an expense provided that the equipment is utilised in the business for a qualifying purpose. In these circumstances, the hirer will not be able to make a claim for capital allowances in respect of the equipment until such time as the option is executed and the liability to pay the option price has been discharged.

Periods equal to the asset's working life

The Revenue may argue that there should be no claim for capital allowances, when the period of the hire purchase contract is so long that there can be no certainty that the market value of the asset at the time of the purchase option will be significantly greater than the option to purchase. Where this is the case, the whole of the rental should be treated as a revenue expense.

Spreading the finance charge throughout the life of the agreement

When the hire purchase contract extends beyond a single accounting period of the hirer, it will be necessary to apportion the finance charge, and the Revenue will usually accept accounts in which either the rule of 78, the actuarial method before tax, or the straight line method have been used, provided that the method chosen is used consistently. The method used need not be the same as that used by the owner.

Capital gains tax

For the purposes of capital gains tax, the asset is treated as being acquired by the hirer at the beginning of the period in which its use is obtained. This applies to both the owner and the hirer although in the usual case, where the owner is trading, this is unlikely to be material to the owner's future position. Any adjustments to the tax position of either party will occur where the agreement ends without property passing to the hirer.

CHAPTER 5

CAPITAL ALLOWANCES AND LEASING TRADES

Plant, machinery and vehicles

Capital allowances are granted in respect of plant and machinery and vehicles acquired by a business and employed wholly and exclusively for the purposes of the trade.

While there is no statutory definition of plant and machinery, the Revenue has conceded that items such as a barrister's library, furniture and fittings and a dry dock are plant and machinery for the purposes of capital allowances. In Yarmouth *v.* France (1887) it was said that plant includes 'whatever apparatus is used by a businessman for carrying on a business, not his stock in trade which he buys or makes for sale; but all goods and chattels, fixed and mobile, living or dead, which he keeps for permanent employment in his business'.

Current rates of allowances

Until 14 March 1984, a business was entitled to deduct 100 per cent of the VAT exclusive price of the asset (excluding motor cars and certain other asset types) in the year of acquisition. With mainstream corporation tax at 52 per cent, this became a very attractive way of deferring the tax liability of a business. It was this opportunity which partly encouraged the expansion of the leasing industry in the United Kingdom between 1973 and 1984.

Following his 1984 Budget speech, the Chancellor introduced a gradual phasing out of first year capital allowances while at the same time reducing the rate of mainstream corporation tax from 52 per cent to the current 35 per cent. Details of this phasing out are given as follows:

Date	*First year capital allowance*
22 March 1972 to 13 March 1984	100 per cent
14 March 1984 to 31 March 1985	75 per cent
1 April 1985 to 31 March 1986	50 per cent
1 April 1986 and thereafter	abolished

From 1 April 1986 the first year allowance was replaced by a writing down allowance calculated at the rate of 25 per cent for each year. The exception remains the private motor car for which allowances are restricted.

Corporation tax rates

A small company pays a reduced rate of corporation tax, currently 25 per cent. The small company is defined for tax purposes by the amount of its profits, and the small companies' rate is applied where the profit does not exceed the lower limit set. Where profits lie between the lower limit and the upper limit (beyond which mainstream corporation tax is payable), a marginal rate applies. This is to allow for the catching up in order that every pound of profit is taxed at the mainstream rate once the upper limit is exceeded.

The Revenue issued a Statement of Practice (SP1/91) on 6 March 1991 which requires that a company must make a claim if it wishes to take advantage of the small companies' rate or marginal relief. Example 5.1 provides an illustration of this.

The thresholds relate to a full year and will be reduced proportionately for shorter accounting periods.

Where a company is a member of a group, the thresholds are divided by the number of associated companies in the group. In deciding how many companies there are in a group for the purposes of the small companies' rate the following apply:

- Dormant companies are ignored,
- Non-resident companies are included,
- Investment and holding companies are included,
- Companies which are associated for any part of the accounting period are included.

A company is an associated company of another if one of the two has control of the other, or both are under the control of the same person or persons.

Example 5.1 Small companies' rate and marginal relief

	Limit up to:		Tax payable:
Year to 31 March 1990			
i.e. £200,000	at 25%	=	£50,000
£800,000	at 37.5%	=	£300,000
and £1,000,000	at 35%	=	£350,000
Year to 31 March 1991			
i.e. £200,000	at 25%	=	£50,000
£800,000	at 36.25%	=	£290,000
and £1,000,000	at 34%	=	£340,000
Year to 31 March 1992			
i.e. £250,000	at 25%	=	£62,500
£1,000,000	at 35%	=	£350,000
and £1,250,000	at 33%	=	£412,500

Tax planning: the marginal rate

It is desirable for an individual company to avoid profits which fall between the lower and the upper limits because the higher marginal rate will be applied to every pound of profit within these limits. To avoid falling into this band, some factors to be considered in relation to capital expenditure which could impact upon the reported profit are the following:

1. The timing of capital allowances.
2. Payment of an enhanced finance (or operating) lease rental. This must be reasonable in trading terms and there can be seen to be commercial benefit. SP3/91 limits the amount of rental enhancements where these are constructed for the purposes of deferring taxation payments.
3. Bringing forward planned capital expenditure and related interest payments.

The Revenue has recognised that such artificial methods of tax deferment exist and have announced the intention to review lease structures, where these are at variance with the historical accounting approach of the lessee, with effect from 11 April 1991.

Calculation of profits

For the purposes of small companies' rate and marginal rate, a company's profits are its trading income, plus any capital gains and any other income chargeable to corporation tax, together with the grossed up amount of any UK dividends receivable other than from fellow group members. A company's capital gains are taxed at the same rate as the company's trading profits.

Any advance corporation tax paid by a company in respect of its distributions (dividends) can be offset against the corporation tax liability arising on the company's total profits including capital gains.

The 25 per cent writing down allowance

The calculation is shown in tabular form as follows:

	Tax written down value (TWDV)	Allowance
Given		
Initial cost	100.00%	—
year 1 (year of acquisition)	75.00%	25.00%
year 2	56.25%	18.75%
year 3	42.19%	14.06%
year 4	31.64%	10.55%
year 5	23.73%	7.91%
year 6	17.80%	5.93%
year 7	13.35%	4.45%
year 8	10.01%	3.34%
year 9	7.51%	2.50%
year 10	5.63%	1.88%
Etc.		

The short life asset election

The new rate of capital allowance for plant and equipment was introduced in an attempt by the government to restrict transactions involving the acquisition of assets simply with a view to deferring tax liability, such transactions lacking substance when applying the test that the equipment must be used wholly and exclusively for the purposes of the trade. In other words, government was seeking to make businesses justify their purchasing decisions from a commercial viewpoint rather than from that of taxation.

However, the phasing out of first year allowances caused potential cashflow problems to companies operating assets for relatively short periods, or operating assets with a short working life. This was recognised in section 57 of the Finance Act 1985 which introduced 'de-pooling' provisions enabling traders to accelerate capital allowances on certain short life machinery or plant, which it is the intention to sell or scrap within five years of its acquisition. The scope of the provisions is not limited to such assets and an election may be made in relation to any machinery or plant which is not specifically excluded elsewhere in legislation.

The mechanism by which this is achieved is the separation of such plant from the general capital allowance pool in which expenditure would otherwise reside. A person wishing to take advantage of the de-pooling provisions must make an election to that effect. The election must be in writing, must specify the assets (referred to as short life assets) concerned, the capital expenditure incurred on those assets and the date on which that capital expenditure was incurred.

There are certain categories of asset which may not be the subject of a de-pooling election and these are the following:

- Ships,
- Motor cars (other than car-derived vans),
- Machinery and plant let other than in the course of a trade,
- Machinery and plant leased abroad and qualifying only for a 10 per cent writing down allowance,
- Cars costing over £8,000.

The short life asset election must be made within two years of the end of the accounting period in which the expenditure was incurred and is irrevocable in respect of that asset once made. If the expenditure on the asset is contracted over a period of time, the two year limit runs from the end of the accounting period in which the first of such expenditure was incurred.

The person making the election must be carrying on a trade, and he or she must have incurred the expenditure on the provision of the assets concerned wholly and exclusively for the purposes of the trade.

To cater for the large volume of assets, some lessors have elected to de-pool all their assets which are not specifically excluded elsewhere in legislation and will then reverse the election should it be considered prudent in the light of the circumstances of specific transactions.

For the calculation of allowances short life assets are treated as follows:

1. The expenditure incurred on short life assets is deemed to be wholly and exclusively incurred for the purpose of a notional trade carried on by the

trader separately from any other trade in which he or she may be engaged. Therefore every short life asset is treated as being in a 'pool' of its own, separate from the general pool of expenditure and any other asset.

2. The notional trade is considered to be permanently discontinued when the short life asset begins to be used wholly or partly for purposes other than those of the actual trade carried on by the trader. If this occurs within the prescribed period, no balancing adjustment is made, but the whole of the tax written down value at the beginning of the period is transferred to the general pool.

3. If the disposal of the short life asset has not occurred by the fourth anniversary of the end of the accounting period in which the expenditure was incurred (or the first expenditure was incurred where there were progress payments), the notional trade is permanently discontinued in the next such accounting period. The tax written down value is then transferred to the general pool of the actual trade.

That is to say, if the asset is sold, scrapped, lost or otherwise disposed of within five years, beginning with the accounting period in which it was acquired, the trader receives a balancing allowance, or balancing charge, immediately on disposal. However, if the asset is still in the trader's possession, and is being used wholly and exclusively for the purposes of the actual trade at the end of the five year period, its tax written down value is transferred to the general pool. The effect of the short life asset election to de-pool is lost, and the tax written down value will be run on at a rate of 25 per cent per annum on a reducing balance basis.

Group relief

Where a lessor company is part of a group, losses arising as a result of the capital allowances may be surrendered to other group companies to be offset against those companies' profits before tax. The company with profits and against which it is intended to set-off the loss is known as the claimant company. Group relief for an accounting period is allowed as a deduction against the claimant company's total profits for the period.

For group relief purposes, an accounting period of a group company claiming relief must at least partly coincide with an accounting period of the group company surrendering the relief (i.e. the dates must overlap). Where the respective accounting dates do not fully coincide, the amount which can be set-off against the total profits of the claimant company for the period will be reduced by the fraction A/B and the total profits of the claimant company will be reduced by the fraction A/C, where A is the length of the accounting

---

Example 5.2 Group relief and the lessor

1.1.90	31.3.90	30.6.90	31.12.90	...	30.9.91

...	company 1	...	(December year-end)	...
...	company 2	...	(December year-end)	...
...	company 3	...	(December year-end)	...
...	company 4	...	(December year-end)	...
				period overlap	

| | 1.10.90 | company 5 | 30.9.91 |

Let us assume that company 5 generates a loss because its capital allowances exceed the profit. The first three months of the trading year of company 5 correspond with the last three months of its group companies (1 to 4). As 'losses' arising by virtue of capital allowances may be carried back twelve months (or carried forward indefinitely), company 5 may, at the end of its trading year, surrender up to 25 per cent of the loss arising by virtue of capital allowances against up to 25 per cent of the total profits of each of companies 1 to 4.

The year-end of company 5 is nine months after the year-end of the other group companies (the date on which they would ordinarily account for the tax on their profits). Provided documentation and business volume is carefully controlled, the effect of group relief will be that the benefit of the capital allowances will become instantly available (i.e. a zero tax delay may be built into the lease pricing structure). This is because one quarter of the available loss may be surrendered to each of the four group companies on the basis that a loss has arisen as a result of the availability of those allowances.

---

period common to both, B is the length of the accounting period of the surrendering company, and C is the length of the accounting period of the claimant company.

For example, if nine months of a twelve month accounting period overlap, the amount which can be set-off against the total profits of the claimant company will be reduced by $9/12$, and the total profits of the claimant company available against which to set-off the amount will also be reduced by $9/12$, assuming both companies account for twelve months of trading.

Group relief and the lessor

This is a particularly important tax planning device for the lessor, since 'losses' arising by virtue of capital allowances may be surrendered (thrown back) against total profits of a group company, thereby accelerating the time when the benefit of the allowances may be brought into the lease cashflow. Example 5.2 illustrates this.

Effect on lease evaluation

As will be seen later, the allowance is treated in the lease evaluation pricing module as if it were a cash sum (the equivalent of a rental), thereby reducing the capital outstanding in the lease, having had due regard for the effect of time on its original value.

Clearly some very detailed assumptions need to be built into the pricing structure and on larger finance lease transactions it will be common to see some form of protection for the lessor covering both changes in the rate of corporation tax and the availability of the allowances at the times specified in the lease cashflows. In the multi-million pound, large value deals, the lease cashflow itself may form an integral part of the documentation for the avoidance of doubt on the part of the parties to the lease.

The basic conditions of entitlement to capital allowances

In any finance leasing contract, the major consideration is likely to be the lessor's entitlement to capital allowances in respect of the capital expenditure in acquiring the plant and equipment which is to be leased. The lessor will, and the lessee should want to, be in a position to be as sure as is reasonably possible that the expenditure will be on a basis which entitles the lessor to the maximum available capital allowances at the most beneficial times during the lease period, in order that the rental and financial costs can be computed accordingly.

Assuming that the equipment to be leased is machinery or plant, the lessor will be required to satisfy various conditions before being entitled to make a claim for capital allowances in respect of the expenditure on the equipment in question. These conditions are principally the following:

1. The lessor must be carrying on a trade which includes the leasing activity.
2. The lessor must actually incur capital expenditure.
3. The capital expenditure must be incurred on the provision of equipment for that actual (or deemed) trade.
4. For the purposes of writing down allowances, the lessor must be able to show that the equipment belongs (or has belonged) to the lessor.

These conditions are now expanded in more detail below.

Carrying on a leasing trade

The trade conducted by an equipment lessor will largely be a question of fact. As a matter of practice, the Revenue rarely argue too strongly that the acquisition of capital equipment for the purpose of leasing should be considered an investment activity rather than a trade.

However, it is always possible that the Revenue may invoke the principle arising in cases such as Lupton v. F.A. and A.B. Limited (1968) 47 TC 580. If trading transactions cannot be said to be trading agreements but are rather, 'an artificial device remote from trade to secure a tax advantage', then those transactions can be struck from the books of the lessor, with the resultant failure of the claim for capital allowances. This is an important point when considering the lease in which no profit could be anticipated were it not for the availability of allowances which were to be taken into account.

The repetitive nature of the transactions accepted by the lessor and the structure of the business, namely the ability not only to write contracts swiftly and efficiently, but also to collect rentals on the due dates and to react effectively in the case of default, will satisfy the Revenue that the badges of trade quintessential of the business of a leasing trade do exist.

Incurring capital expenditure

There is nothing in legislation to define what is meant by incurring capital expenditure, only the definition of the time when expenditure is incurred, or considered to be incurred. The word incurring cannot be equated with the actual expenditure of funds by the lessor, but simply relates to the contractual commitment to acquire capital equipment in return for a consideration. This is consistent with the Capital Allowances Act, which suggests that a person incurring capital expenditure does so when a contractual commitment to acquire capital equipment from a vendor is established.

It is therefore necessary only to enter into a contract for the supply of equipment, in a manner such that there is no element of doubt as to the intended performance of that contract, in order to establish that the capital expenditure has taken place. Revenue practice will be to look at the date of the invoice relating to the sale.

If the date of the invoice is the last day of the financial year, but a period of, say, thirty days is given as standard trade terms before settlement is required, then that expenditure will be deemed to have been incurred within the financial year, provided that the consideration for the purchase is met within the period of thirty days' grace.

Capital expenditure on the provision of equipment

Is expenditure on the provision of equipment deemed to be capital or revenue? The expenditure incurred in the character of a genuine leasing trade will be of a capital nature, but the person acquiring an asset, with a view to its short-term hire and subsequent disposal at a profit, may be required to treat that expenditure as revenue.

This problem may arise where the lessor of equipment also wishes to include the activities of buying and selling the equipment in the business in question. Should a prospective lessor control an existing business which encompasses the buying and selling of the equipment which it is wished to lease, the prospective lessor may be well advised to establish a separate company for the purposes of the leasing activity.

The equipment which is subject to a finance lease will normally be sold at the expiry of the lease, with the lessee being appointed as the agent of the lessor for the purposes of the disposal. The lessee will often be entitled to retain the lion's share of the sale proceeds, either as a rebate of rentals or as a sales agency commission. The fact that the lessor is bound from the outset to sell the equipment has not caused an argument by the Revenue that the lessor's original expenditure was revenue in nature.

The revenue hypothesis may prove difficult to substantiate because the sale will often not take place for a considerable period of time (and may not take place at all if the equipment has ultimately only a scrap value). Additionally, there will generally be no specifically identified purchaser until the sale itself has been concluded. Finally, since the lessor will retain only a small percentage of the sale proceeds, it will be clear that the bulk of the lessor's profit has arisen out of rental income rather than profit from resale.

The lessor will generally limit the amount of the sale proceeds that will be shared by way of a rental rebate. If this is not the case it could otherwise be argued that, should the rebate of rentals exceed the rentals paid by the lessee during the lease term, the lessor will not have earned sufficient income from the equipment to authenticate the claim that the purpose of the investment was to generate profit out of rental income.

Other capital expenditure considerations deal with the provision of plant or machinery. Some of these considerations are outlined as follows:

1. *Preparatory and incidental expenditure*: In order to qualify for capital allowances the expenditure must be incurred on the provision of the

equipment. Expenditure which is preparatory or incidental to such provision may be expected to qualify for allowances as being a part of the expenditure incurred on the provision of the equipment as a whole. Alterations to buildings which are properly incidental to the installation, such as ducting, cabling and wiring, are specifically permitted for the purposes of the legislation.

2. *Delivery and installation*: Delivery and installation costs relating to the equipment will usually be acceptable for allowances. However, the costs incurred in arranging the finance for the asset (although these may be capitalised in the lessor's books of account) will not be taken as expenditure on the provision of the asset, but rather as expenditure on the provision of the finance, and will therefore not qualify for allowances.

3. *Advance, or progress, payments*: Where stage payments are made, the lessor will usually want to claim the allowances for each payment as soon as is possible. At the point during construction of the equipment when such payments are made, the item may not be sufficiently complete to be described as plant or machinery; the construction may not have commenced should the first payment be required at the time of placing the order. This will not usually prevent an allowance claim, since the substance of the underlying contract is the utlimate supply of the finished equipment. It is this, rather than the current physical state, which will determine whether the expenditure is incurred on the provision of the plant or machinery. Until 1 April 1985, it was a requirement of a claim for writing down allowances that the equipment should have been brought into use before such a claim could be made. This was in contrast to a claim in respect of a first year allowance, and Finance Act 1985 introduced new legislation reflecting the fact that first year allowances were to be phased out following the provision in the Finance Act of the previous year.

Plant or machinery belonging to the lessor

Where assets are installed in buildings provision, in the context of an allowance claim, does not necessarily suggest a proprietary interest in the asset, but for a claim for allowances to be valid the equipment must belong to the lessor. There is no definition laid down by statute as to what does and what does not constitute belonging in this context, and complications can arise where the lease is for fixed equipment installed in a building.

Although the lessor may enter into supplementary documentation, such as a joint election to the effect that only the lessor may make a valid claim for capital allowances, or a landlord's waiver in respect of the interest in the equipment, the lessor may find there is difficulty in pursuing a claim for allowances where the asset is permanently fixed within a building. This is because the lessor will be unable to satisfy the Revenue that a leasing trade has been established in respect of the equipment.

In law, it is well established that merely turning land into account for an income is not a trading activity, and the situation would not change just because that land happened to have some fixed assets attached to it. The lessor may on occasion take a leasehold interest in the land, where, in so doing, the success of a claim for allowances, in respect of equipment or buildings placed on it, can be assured as a result.

A further difficulty with assets belonging to the lessor arises where the lessor has contracted to sell the equipment to a specific third party on the termination of the lease. This may be exacerbated where the third party was the original supplier, and the sale at the end of the lease term has the effect of a 'repurchase' of the asset. This is because it could be argued that the equipment did not belong beneficially to the lessor, even though the third party might not be the beneficial owner during the period of the lease. To relieve this possible area of doubt, the lessor will generally draw up the repurchase agreement in a form of words that leave an option to avoid the sale, along the lines of 'if called upon in writing so to do . . .'.

Exceptions to the rules of belonging

There is a major exception to the general rule that equipment must belong to the person who is intending to claim capital allowances. This occurs where expenditure is incurred under a contract which provides that the claimant shall become the owner on the performance of the contract.

Two important consequences are provided for. The first is that the equipment is reckoned to belong to the party who is entitled to the benefit of the contract at any time during which this party is so entitled. Second, all future capital expenditure under the same contract is deemed to be incurred as soon as the equipment is brought into use. As a result, the lessor acquiring goods by means of hire purchase or conditional sale is able to claim capital allowances in respect of the equipment immediately. Equally, the first point will be of assistance to the lessor who wishes to make an immediate claim in respect of equipment which is being supplied by means of stage payments.

For the lessor to claim allowances, expenditure must be incurred in a manner wherein the contract allows for the lessor to become the owner when all the conditions have been satisfied (i.e. on the performance of the contract). There is no requirement for an assessment of the state of the equipment during a construction period, or the amount of the stage payments which may be allowed for capital allowance purposes, provided the conditions relating to the ultimate acquisition of ownership are satisfied. Provisions were introduced to remove the necessity to wait for an asset to be brought into use before a claim for writing down allowances could be made with effect from 1 April 1985. This followed the phasing out of first year allowances for which this requirement was anyway unnecessary.

The benefits of deferred purchase methods

The advantages of accelerating the capital allowances have encouraged a number of lessors to turn to this method of funding their assets out on lease. This is because of the minimal capital outlay required on the inception of the hire purchase contract, and the fact that the profiles of the two rental structures can usually be matched in an advantageous way to the lessor's cashflow, when the capital allowances are taken into account.

Potential difficulties with matched cashflows

Non-recourse finance

Difficult problems can arise when transactions are structured in such a way that the cashflows from the hire purchase arrangement and the lease match exactly. This is particularly relevant where the hire purchase lessor charges or assigns the lease to the supplier, so that the hire purchase contract fails to be of a non-recourse nature. The supplier will rely upon the payment of the lease rentals to secure the payment of the hire purchase instalments. The liability of the lessor will be limited to making hire purchase payments only out of rentals actually received. In this type of agreement, there is the danger that the Revenue will question the fact that the lessor actually incurs expenditure at all.

In practice, apart from the hybrid type of agreement (referred to in the previous paragraph), it will be generally accepted that, for the purposes of capital allowances, it is the cash price shown on the hire purchase agreement which will be the reference point for deciding the amount of capital expenditure incurred, rather than the price of the option to purchase.

Option price and market value

It is important that the option price is less than market value, otherwise there is the risk that the Revenue will argue that the hire purchase instalments were merely payment for the use of the asset, rather than a payment towards the option to purchase. For this reason, the hire purchase period should be less than the useful working life of the asset, in order that the market value remains significantly higher than the option to purchase.

Final balloon payments

It will become apparent that care needs to be taken in structuring hire purchase contracts where a balloon, or large option to purchase, is payable, in order to secure the available capital allowances of the hirer.

The exception of credit sale

It is of note that while these provisions apply to conditional sale and hire purchase, a credit sale transaction, permitting the lessor to make payment of the purchase price by instalments, will not qualify for writing down allowance purposes until the actual payments themselves are made. In other words there will be no acceleration of capital allowances even though title to the goods has passed immediately.

Notes

Some notes on capital allowances are as follows:

1. Writing down allowances are available even though an asset is disposed of without being brought into use, provided that it can be shown that the original expenditure was incurred for the purposes of the trade. Where the disposal occurs during the same accounting period as the acquisition, it is the difference between the cost of the asset, less the sale proceeds on disposal, which will be added (or deducted) from the pool.
2. Strictly, for an individual only, only the allowances required should be claimed, whereas for a company, allowances will be given in full unless they are specifically disclaimed.
3. Only machinery and plant not specified in section 38 of the Capital Allowances Act 1990 are eligible to be treated as short life assets. Where it is impractical to identify individual short life assets, a form of pooling may be adopted (Revenue Statement of Practice SP1/86).
4. Where an asset is leased to a non-UK resident for the purposes of overseas trade the writing down allowance will be restricted to a

maximum rate of 10 per cent per annum. Such expenditure will form a separate pool under Section 41 of the Capital Allowances Act 1990 by virtue of it falling within setion 42 (assets leased outside the United Kingdom).

Restriction of capital allowances for private motor cars

Private motor cars are subject to a restriction of the capital allowance available. When the purchase price, inclusive of car tax and VAT, exceeds £8,000, the allowance will be restricted to 25 per cent of the first £8,000, or to £2,000 per annum (whichever is the less). Upon disposal the balancing charge or allowance will be brought into account at the date of disposal, and for this reason it is necessary to create a separate 'expensive motor car pool' for each and every vehicle costing in excess of £8,000.

CHAPTER 6

PROVISION FOR TAXATION WITHIN LEASE DOCUMENTATION

Introduction

The lessor's view of the lease will be that of an investment on which it will be expected to receive a financial return. The lease document will therefore include safeguards, which protect the lessor in the event of third party claims, and which will state the actions which may be taken in the event of a default in payment by the lessee.

Tax variation clauses

There will generally be provision for the lessor's protection against movement in taxation conditions which may affect the lease cashflow. Where there is a tax variation clause, this will set out the assumptions on which the rentals have been calculated. In addition, reference will be made to the basis upon which adjustments can be made to the rental stream, in order that the lessor's post-tax financial position will be ultimately reinstated.

Frequently there will be a reference not only to additional rentals which may fall due, but also to the opportunity for some form of rental rebate, where taxation conditions move in favour of the lessor, who will in turn share that benefit with the lessee to a greater or lesser extent.

Several alternatives exist for the lessor. The most common assumptions to which reference may be made are as follows:

1. Alteration to the rate of capital allowances.
2. Change of use.
3. Loss of allowances through lessor error.
4. Changes in the rate of corporation tax.
5. Alteration to the accounting basis.
6. Changes in accounting period or tax payment dates.
7. The treatment of rental rebates.

54

Alteration to the rate of capital allowances

The lessor will state the assumption that he or she will expect to 'obtain and retain' capital allowances in respect of expenditure on the assets which are subject to the lease, and that those allowances will be available to the lessor for the accounting period in which the expenditure is incurred.

Change of use

In addition, the assumption will generally be drawn to provide the lessor with protection should the lessee cease to use the equipment for qualifying purposes. The clause will be extended to cover use in such a manner as to render the lessor to receive allowances at a lower rate. Special provisions may be included when the lessor has agreed to a subletting of the equipment.

This can present quite difficult problems when, for example, the lease is a joint lease, and the availability of allowances depends on the status of each of the lessees. For instance, the residential status of partners in a partnership can cause questions, should there be a change in the profit sharing ratios of the partners during the term of the lease.

Loss of allowances through lessor error

The lessee ought to ascertain that the documentation excludes the lessee's liability to make good the loss of capital allowances by virtue of actions by the lessor. The documentation should cover loss of allowances either by the lessor's error, mistake or by voluntary disclaimer of all or part of the allowance during any accounting period. In other words, the lessee's liability to pay additional rentals should be limited only to statutory changes outside the control of the lessor.

Both parties will need to quantify the amount of the expenditure which is to be subject to a claim for allowances. Both should be agreed upon the timing of the expenditure when the lessor is to be called upon to provide progress, or advance, payments over which the lessee will have an element of control.

Changes in the rate of corporation tax

The lessor will state that the assumption has been made that a rate of corporation tax has been used to generate the rentals, and this rate will remain unchanged throughout the lease cashflow. There will usually be a stipulation for adjustments to be made in favour of the lessee where the changes in the tax rates favour the lessor's cashflow, and this type of clause is known as a 'two-way' tax clause.

Alteration to the accounting basis

The lessor may wish to obtain protection against changes in Inland Revenue practice relating to the accounting basis used in preparing the lease cashflows. The accruals basis has been generally accepted by lessors as the method for apportioning rentals to their respective accounting periods. Some lessors have, however, used cash-based accounting in order to favour structures in which rentals are to be paid on an arrears basis.

This area is currently under review by the Revenue. In a Statement of Practice dated 11 April 1991, the Revenue published its intended future approach to the payment of rentals by the lessee. In due course, it is to be expected that the Revenue will state its views on the cash accounting methods employed by lessors. In anticipation of this, there has been a recent move towards accrual accounting by some of the cash accounting lessors, and cash-based accounting now remains an approach used only by a small number of insurance company owned lessors.

Changes in accounting period or tax payment dates

There may be provision for the lessor to have protection should some statutory measure alter the dates on which the allowances are to be paid, or the tax on the rental inflows is to fall due. The lessee would be well advised to insist that any such provision should only become effective in respect of statutory changes as opposed to voluntary actions taken by the lessor.

The treatment of rental rebates

There will often be allowance for a single payment by way of an indemnity, in the event that the lessor is unable to claim payment of a rebate of rentals (or a sales agency commission) as an expense in the accounting period in which that payment is made. The treatment of the lessee's responsibility as an indemnity is preferable, as it will arise upon the settlement of the lease when the opportunity for a final, or additional, compensating rental will no longer apply. This might prove to be particularly important should the rebate of rentals exceed the rental payments which have been made by the lessee.

Summary

The lessor will seek to preserve a post-tax rate of return from the lease. Many of the provisions will be the subject of detailed negotiation in the large value transaction. In low value agreements, there will often be some simple formulae within the lease documentation. These will provide for swift and easy adjustment to rental streams following changes in conditions relating to specific assumptions. The lessee should be satisfied that these adjustments are equitable, and that they apply in the event of circumstances favouring the lease cashflow, thereby allowing adjustment in favour of the lessee in such a case.

Where the rental has been calculated to reflect the benefit of a short life asset election, the lessee may wish to quantify the cashflow effect, in the event that the asset has to be sold at a value equal to or greater than its tax written down value.

CAPITAL ALLOWANCES AND FOREIGN LEASING

Introduction

The reduced rates of capital allowances which apply to equipment used by foreign end-users do not apply where the equipment is to be used only outside the United Kingdom. Where an asset is located within the United Kingdom, but used by a non-resident who is not using the equipment for UK trading purposes, the allowances will be restricted, or possibly withdrawn completely.

Notional writing down allowances of 10 per cent per annum will be available by virtue of section 42 of the Capital Allowances Act 1990 to a lessor who leases an asset to a non-resident lessee for the purposes of that lessee's trade in the country of residence.

Where the lessor has previously leased the asset to a UK resident trading company and claimed writing down allowances at a rate of 25 per cent as a result, a balancing charge will arise. This charge will be equal to the tax written down value (known as the residue of expenditure), plus the balancing charge. The balancing charge, itself, will be equal to the excess of actual allowances (at 25 per cent WDA basis) over the notional allowances (at 10 per cent).

Example 6.1. provides an illustration of capital allowances and foreign leasing.

Example 6.1. Capital allowances and foreign leasing

A lessor enters into a lease with X Limited, a company trading in the United Kingdom, in respect of equipment costing £20,000. During the third year, the lessee terminates the lease and the lessor then enters into a contract to lease the equipment with a South American company for the purposes of its trade there. The new lessee is a foreign resident.

Actual allowances		*Total allowances*
	£	£
Year 1	20,000	
WDA at 25%	(5,000)	5,000
Year 2	15,000	
WDA at 25%	(3,750)	3,750
Year 3	11,250	
WDA at 25%	(2,813)	2,813
Residue of expenditure	8,437	
	Total allowances claimed	11,563

Notional allowances		*Total allowances*
	£	£
Year 1	20,000	
WDA at 10%	(2,000)	2,000
Year 2	18,000	
WDA at 10%	(1,800)	1,800
Year 3	16,200	
WDA at 10%	(1,620)	1,620
	14,580	
	Notional allowances	5,420

A balancing charge will arise which is equal to the excess of the actual allowances over the notional allowances in the year in which the new lease is incepted:

	£
Actual allowances	11,563
Notional allowances	5,420
Balancing charge	6,143

The lessor will be reckoned to have incurred expenditure of £14,580 which is made up of the residue of expenditure and the balancing charge. This will arise in the year following the year in which the change of use occurred.

	£
Residue of expenditure	8,437
Balancing charge	6,143
Expenditure incurred	14,580

Writing down allowances at 10 per cent per annum will be claimed in respect of this expenditure, and this cost will be retained in a separate pool for the purposes of section 41 of the Capital Allowances Act 1990.

Summary

The area of foreign leasing is potentially complicated. It will however be noted that the lessor will need to pay special attention to the underlying tax position when considering the supply of lease facilities to non-resident lessees.

It is to be expected that the lease documentation will contain clauses which deal with a change in the residential status of the lessee during the lease term.

THE IMPACT OF VALUE ADDED TAX

Leasing

For VAT purposes leasing is accounted for as a supply of services and therefore the periodic lease rentals will be subject to VAT at the rate which is current at the tax point date.

VAT on equipment lease rentals will be charged at the standard rate except in the following cases:

1. The leasing of goods for use outside the United Kingdom throughout the period of the lease where the equipment is either exported out of the United Kingdom by the lessor, or is not in the United Kingdom at the date of supply, in which case the rentals will be zero rated.
2. Various items in the transport group (Group 10 schedule 5, Valued Added Tax Act 1983); this includes the supply of any ship of gross tonnage which is less than 15 tons, and the supply of any aircraft of less

than 8,000 kg which have not been adapted for use for pleasure or recreation. In which case the rentals will be zero rated.

Limitations to input tax credit

No credit is allowed for the input tax chargeable on the supply of a private motor car (although there are exceptions such as the Motability scheme), but the VAT chargeable on the rentals will be recoverable.

The lessor may be prevented from obtaining full credit for input tax if part of the business involves making exempt supplies.

Disposal and early termination

Customs and Excise will normally accept that any payment made by a lessee on early settlement of a lease should be treated as a supply of services by the lessor to the lessee and should therefore be liable to VAT.

Where the equipment is sold at the end of the lease (or on the termination if earlier), Customs and Excise do not in practice require the lessee to account for the VAT, provided there is no VAT on any invoice issued by the lessee. The rebate of rental, or the sales agency commission, are effectively disregarded for VAT purposes where the payments are made between lessor and lessee. However, where a third party is concerned the treatment of VAT will depend upon the individual circumstances.

Hire purchase

The transfer of possession of goods under a hire purchase agreement is treated as the supply of goods. The tax point date will be the date when the goods are made available to the recipient. If a tax invoice is issued, or payment is received prior to this date, then it is this date which becomes the tax point date.

The finance charge within a hire purchase document will be exempt from VAT where it is disclosed separately to the hirer with the cash price of the goods being standard rated. The export of equipment will be zero rated, and the provisions of the treatment of equipment in the transport group referred to above will apply under hire purchase, credit or conditional sale.

The hirer may generally expect the financier to require the VAT element of the contract to fall payable upon signing of the contract. The hirer will then usually be able to reclaim that VAT as an input at the next accounting date.

CHAPTER 7

DOCUMENTATION

Introduction

Within the discussion of taxation matters, we highlighted the importance of protection to the parties within the lease contract. Whichever product is selected the documentation will form a fundamental part of any financing transaction. It should protect the interests of both the user and the financier. Otherwise, lack of completeness may have serious consequences to either or both parties later on.

The facility letter

The customer will generally expect the financier to offer an enforceable commitment to provide the required facilities at the time they are needed. Often the funding will cover a range of assets over a period of time, sometimes with the complication of stage payments, and it will be necessary to indicate the terms and conditions attaching to the transaction before the full documentation is produced.

Some points to consider include the following:

1. The customer will expect the facility letter to create a binding commitment on the financier to provide facilities subject to fulfilment of certain obligations by the customer.
2. The letter will specify precisely what security may be required, together with a firm indication of the costs involved in perfecting that security.
3. The financier will wish to limit the time scale during which the offer of finance will remain open and will define the amount of any fees payable upon acceptance.

Leasing facilities

Introduction

The speed with which many of the smaller leasing transactions will be accommodated may circumvent the production of a formal facility letter. Many lessors now handle modest sized transactions on single sheet, self-duplicating documentation, containing the terms of the transaction on one side and the conditions on the reverse.

Large contracts, or facilities relating to a number of assets to be acquired over a period of time, will however often be the subject of a formal facility letter.

The leasing agreement

The standard leasing agreement, which will be in a preprinted form, will contain all the general terms and conditions to accommodate the whole range of the assets in which the lessor is prepared to deal. The lessor who is prepared to deal in high value transactions will usually be willing to negotiate certain variations to such a document to the extent that special conditions will be required in respect of assets such as ships, aircraft and major installations.

Standard terms in lease documents

Details of some standard terms used in lease documents are given below:

1. *Corporation tax*: Some leases will not allow for changes in corporation tax assumptions. This will tend to occur in short-term vehicle hire, television and video hire, and some low value asset leases. The majority of contracts should include provision for changes in the rate of corporation tax, and for an indemnity by the lessee to the lessor should actions on behalf of the lessee prejudice a claim for capital allowances.

2. *The master lease principle*: Where the lessee seeks financial accommodation for a range of assets over a period of time, the lease documentation will generally take the form of a master lease incorporating all the general terms which will govern subsequent lease transactions. Individual assets (or groups of assets to be acquired at the same time and leased on similar terms) will then be incorporated in schedules, which are drawn up to relate back to the master lease document containing the principal terms and conditions. The master lease is an active document, since it creates and controls the terms of

the subsequent hirings, and it should always be dated prior to the date of the first schedule. Should this not be the case, any schedules perfected prior to that date will be outside its control.

3. *Creation of the hiring*: The lease agreement will contain an agreement to hire the goods, defining not only the duration of the period of hire but also the rental structure over the total period. There will be an agreement to pay rentals which will generally be treated to be the 'essence' of the contract, since failure by the lessor to achieve a commercial return on funds employed may render a claim for allowances to be refuted by the Revenue.

4. *Covenants by the lessee*: The lessee's responsibilities under the terms of a finance lease will normally extend to the following:

1. Providing adequate maintenance for the asset.
2. Providing adequate insurance against loss and third party claims.
3. Taking due care of the asset and permitting its operation only by suitably qualified persons.
4. Paying all taxes and to obtaining all licences in respect of its use.
5. Returning the asset or disposing of it in accordance with the lessor's instruction at the end of the period of hire.
6. Notifying the lessor in the event of adverse trading results affecting the business of the lessee.
7. Providing indemnities against liabilities arising from the use of the asset.

The lessee may also be required to provide indemnities to the lessor, in respect of loss of capital allowances arising on change of use of the asset, or on the change of residential status of one or more of the principles of the lessee's business.

There will also be clauses which define what is considered to be an action of default by the lessee, and the remedies available to the lessor in such an event.

The contract will include general clauses which specify the governing law, the basis upon which notices can be served and various definitions, as follows:

1. *The provision of adequate maintenance*: The lessee will be expected to maintain and service the asset in accordance with the manufacturer's recommendations. While safety of operation will be a primary concern of any responsible lessor, the lessor is afforded a degree of protection should repossession occur as a result of a default and the value of the asset fail to reflect fair wear and tear. The lessor may then have some redress against the lessee to make good any loss which results from the failure of the lessee to

fulfil the responsibilities under the contract. Such a clause will also serve to confirm that the lessor under a finance lease gives no covenant to repair, maintain or otherwise replace the asset. The lessee will still have an obligation to pay rentals even though denied the use of the asset until such time as it may be declared a total loss. The lessee will be expected to keep an adequate record of maintenance carried out on the asset and to make this record available for inspection by the lessor following a reasonable period of notice.

2. *The provision of adequate insurance*: The lessor will expect that insurance will cover both loss or destruction of the asset at its full replacement value, as well as third party claims. The insurance will need to be taken out either when delivery is accepted by the lessee or when the risk would otherwise pass to the lessor, with the proviso that the lessor will generally reserve the right to specify some other date should that be justified by the circumstances.

The insurance will frequently note the lessor's interest. Many lessors require a form of written confirmation that insurance has been effected, not only prior to paying for the equipment, but at certain annual review dates during the period of the hiring.

When leasing ships or aircrafts, the lessor will need to be a joint insured, and a 'loss payee clause' will need to be incorporated into the documentation because of the potentially large sums involved.

There will be provision requiring additional cover to be acquired where modifications to the asset have taken place. There should be a definition of a formula to arrive at the payment of a monetary sum due to the lessor in the event of a total loss of the asset. Generally this should be based upon a formula geared to the discounted outstanding rentals less insurance monies received.

3. *Care and operation of the asset*: It is usual to find that the lessee will be required to make several covenants regarding the use and operation of the asset. Not only will these include the area of maintenance, but the lessor will need to agree to any subsequent modification, since this may have an impact upon the ultimate title to the asset as a whole. The lessor will need to be satisfied that the asset will continue to be used for the purpose for which it was designed, and in such a way that no employment laws will be contravened, nor insurance policies invalidated. It is to be expected that the lessor will want the right to inspect the equipment following a reasonable period of notice.

4. *The payment of taxes*: The lessor will wish to provide that the lessee will be responsible for all taxes, including vehicle excise duties, under the terms of a finance lease.

5. *The lessor's requirements at termination*: The lessor will need to build in provision for the control of the disposal of the asset at the end of the lease term. This will arise because of the allowance claim in respect of the asset and also because of the potential costs for which the lessor could be liable if the asset were to be improperly scrapped.

6. *Notification of adverse trading*: Where an expenditure programme is to extend over a period of time, the lessee will be required to notify the lessor of adverse factors affecting the trading performance. The lessor will then be able to reassess the commitment to provide further facilities although, generally speaking, the lessor will be unable to withdraw from the existing contracts while the lessee's responsibilities continue to be performed by the lessee.

7. *Indemnities arising from use of the asset*: The lessor will require protection for the potential loss should the lessee take some action which would cause the lessor to fail to obtain all or part of the capital allowances which were built into the lease evaluation. This will apply in circumstances such as the asset no longer being used for UK trading activity, resulting in a reduction in the value of the capital allowances.

Title to the asset

The lease will need to refer to title remaining with the lessor at all times, in order that the lessor may claim capital allowances. The lessee's rights will therefore be limited to the use of the asset for the period of the lease.

It is a common practice for the lessor to insist upon the right to attach a plate indicating ownership to the leased asset, although for reasons of cost this is rarely done other than in cases of serious default. There will however be restrictions upon the lessee's right to dispose of the asset without the lessor's prior written agreement.

Warranties and indemnities

The lessor will draw up the contract in a manner which attempts to exclude any obligation other than to allow 'the quiet possession of the asset for the term of the lease'.

A finance lease will often provide for the assignment of all rights to warranties to the lessee, so that the lessee may then deal directly with the original supplier in respect of the condition, or operation, of the goods.

The lessee will generally be expected to indemnify the lessor against a wide range of potential costs applying to the operation of the asset. These will include maintenance and repair, as well as infringement of copyrights and patents, and third party claims resulting from its leasing use or operation.

Penalty interest rates

The lessor will wish to include a clause allowing for additional rentals to be charged based upon interest calculations in respect of rentals which are overdue. The margin over the cost of funds applied may be as high as 5 or 6 per cent, although this is generally in line with charges applied by clearing banks and other lending institutions in similar circumstances.

Termination

The lessor will seek to define the circumstances which will give rise to a termination, the lessor's rights in such event, and the sums which may then be payable both to the lessee and the lessor. The lessor's right to terminate will include default by the lessee, breach of the conditions of the lease, and, depending upon the drafting, the lessee's default of some other agreement in which the lessor had a declared interest.

There will often be a fairly complex calculation allowing for the lessor to claim damages in the event of a default by the lessee, together with a statement of the lessor's rights to deal with the goods to minimise any loss in the event of such a default.

The return of the goods

The way in which the goods are to be returned at the end of the contract term, and the manner in which they are to be sold, will be set out in this clause.

Assignment of rights

The lessor will wish to include a clause to prevent the lessee assigning the agreement or subletting the goods without the prior consent of the lessor. The lessor will generally reserve the right of assignment, but this will usually be limited to an assignment within the lessor's own trading group.

General points

There will be provision for information to be given to the lessor on the state of the assets; details of how notices are to be served between lessor and lessee; and a statement to the effect that the lease is to be controlled by the law of England (Scotland, etc.).

The structure of the lease

1. *The master lease and schedule*: Larger value transactions, and those contracts relating to multiple assets acquired over a period of time, will be governed by a master lease and subsequent schedules. The master lease will be signed by both parties before the purchasing programme commences and will contain all the terms and conditions relating to the conduct of the lessor and the lessee.

The lease schedule will create the hiring of specific assets under the control of the master lease document. Primarily, it will be concerned with identifying the goods, and stating the rates and period of the individual transaction. In many cases there will be a separate bank mandate for each schedule, although lessors will sometimes be prepared to collect rentals for more than one schedule under one bank mandate.

The schedule will be identified by a unique number and its date will be later than that of the master lease document. Invoices will be attached to the schedule where there is a detailed description of the assets. Wherever possible serial numbers will be listed in order to avoid confusion should there be a subsequent dispute.

2. *The 'one-shot' lease*: Small transactions will frequently be accommodated by a single document on which the schedule will appear on the front and the lease terms and conditions on the reverse. In such cases, conditions such as those relating to variation of taxation conditions will often be simplified.

Summary

The lease documentation will be drafted to provide the lessee with the maximum benefits of the use of the asset, while maintaining the principle that ownership remains with the lessor. The function of the finance lease lessor is to provide the funds and the taxable capacity. All responsibility for the operation of the assets will remain with the lessee, who will be permitted the exclusive use of them during the term of the lease.

Areas of the Consumer Credit Act may impact on the lease and the lessor's responsibilities where the customer is an unincorporated body.

Obtaining good title to leased assets

A good title to the leased assets must be established for the purposes of claiming capital allowances and for the right of the lessee to quiet possession to be assured. There are four possible routes to obtaining good title and these are as follows:

1. Direct purchase.
2. Agency purchase.
3. Sale and leaseback.
4. Novation.

Direct purchase

Direct purchase is the simplest method. The lessee submits a personally signed lease to the lessor, and the supplier submits a sale contract (which has been signed by the supplier) to the lessor. In this way the lessor avoids a commitment to purchase until a lease is established. These documents form the basis of an offer by the supplier to supply the goods, and the basis of an offer by the lessee to lease them on the terms and conditions in the leasing document.

The goods will have been delivered and the lessee will be required to certify that payment should be made by the lessor, thereby overcoming any possible conflict as to who the owner will be once payment has been made. It should be possible for the lessee to instruct the lessor to hold a retention of the lessee's payment for goods, subject to the performance of some specific responsibility of the supplier, and stage payments may be negotiated subject to some additional documentation.

In transactions of very high value (such as those for ships), the lessor will make a commitment to the acquisition of the asset upon completion, and the lessee will then be appointed to supervise the construction. The lessee will also be committed to lease the asset when construction is finished, or to compensate the lessor should the lessee fail to do so for any reason. Although there is some element of risk for the lessor in this approach, the covenant of the lessee will be considered to be undoubted because of the magnitude of the transaction and the substance of the lessee.

Agency purchase

The lessor may agree to appoint the lessee as the agent to acquire assets which the lessee will then agree to lease from the lessor. There is a disadvantage to the lessor with this in so far as control over the expenditure is lost and the lessee may exceed the authority contained within the agency appointment document. Generally, the lessor will restrict agency appointments to well established lessees for this reason.

There are three forms of agency, as follows:

1. Disclosed: this may be attractive when the lessee wishes to advertise the association with the lessor in a sales-aid scheme.
2. Undisclosed sole agency: the lessor appoints one company to acquire assets which are agreed in advance. This may apply for a group of assets, for a large item such as a computer installation employing a number of different suppliers, or where the asset is to be imported in a foreign currency.
3. Undisclosed multiple agency: this may occur when a group of companies wish to acquire and lease assets through different subsidiary companies at different times of the year. To the lessee, the principle benefit of the undisclosed agency is that it leaves the buying programme unaltered and does not reveal the lessee's funding arrangements to its suppliers. The major disadvantage to the lessor remains that of lack of control. Expenditure programmes can frequently over run, and it can be difficult to distinguish goods between competing agencies.

In order to overcome the potential confusion when several lessors compete for the same asset types, the lessor will generally require to be presented with the original receipted invoices which have been satisfied by the lessee before drawing up a lease contract within an agency arrangement. The agency should be established before an order for the goods is placed by the lessee.

Sale and leaseback

Sale and leaseback can prove to be a simple route for the lessor to obtain good title to leased assets. Upon agreement, the lessee will raise an invoice on the lessor, at the same time assuring the lessor that title is available to be passed upon completion. The lessor will benefit since there will be no supplier to go through. However, the lessor will probably wish to investigate the value placed upon the asset, when there is a protracted period between the date when the lessee acquired it and the date of the proposed sale and leaseback.

The lessor will usually insist upon receiving the lessee's original receipted invoice before settling the sale and leaseback invoice. In this way the lessor will gain some protection regarding a possible conflict of title, or double financing of the asset.

Novation agreements

The novation will often take place by means of simple letters of agreement being drawn up between the lessor, the lessee and the supplier, wherein the lessor requests being invoiced by the supplier following delivery of the goods. This is significant with items such as computer installations, because the lessee maintains a direct relationship with the supplier until the point when title is due to pass and will be able to negotiate favourable warranties. Additionally, the lessor only becomes committed to purchase when the lessee is satisfied with the goods.

Although a variation of the direct purchase method, a novation agreement is a substitution of a new contract for an old contract in consideration of the discharge of the old contract. In the leasing context, the new contract will have different parties. Computer suppliers prefer this type of arrangement because the lessee remains bound to the supplier for matters such as installation, the lessor only being substituted in respect of taking title in return for payment.

It will be important that the parties draw up the novation in such a way that it is a full substitution of one contract for another and not simply an assignment of the old contract. Stamp duty would be payable in the latter case.

Hire purchase facilities

Introduction

Hire purchase (or lease purchase as it is sometimes described) is a hiring with the option to purchase the asset at the end of the term. Speed of service will often mean that a facility letter is not produced and many financiers handle small transactions by way of single sheet documentation. Larger expenditure programmes may be subject to a formal facility letter. The customer will expect this letter to create an enforceable commitment on the financier to provide funds when required. It will contain similar details to a leasing facility letter.

The hiring agreement

The standard document will be in preprinted form and will contain all the terms and conditions of the hiring. The structure of the documentation will depend on the size and the complexity of the transaction and will either comprise a master hire purchase agreement and schedules, or a single sheet document.

The basic terms concerning the use of the equipment will follow from the leasing narrative above, except that there will be no reference to tax variations, since the hirer will have the right to any available tax benefits.

Where a master document exists, this will control the terms and conditions of individual transactions, and the schedules will establish the individual hirings, detailing the specific terms upon which they have been created.

The option to purchase

There will be a clause describing the circumstances upon which the hirer can execute the option to purchase, either at the end of the agreement or upon early termination.

Acquisition of title

A sale and hire purchase-back is not possible because such a transaction would in effect become a loan against security rather than a hiring. However, it is possible for good title of the financier to be obtained by any of the other routes already described for leasing, which are the following:

1. Direct purchase.
2. Agency purchase.
3. Novation.

Summary

The additional points discussed for leasing will generally apply to hire purchase.

Guarantees and indemnities

Introduction

Guarantees and indemnities are different forms of contracts of security. In most cases the financier will attempt to perfect its additional security both as a guarantee and an indemnity.

The guarantee

A contract of guarantee will be between three parties: the creditor (the financier), the principal debtor (the lessee, the borrower, or the hirer) and the surety (the guarantor). Liability remains with the lessee and the guarantor will only become liable if the principal debtor fails to perform the debtor's obligations under the principal contract. A contract of guarantee must be in writing, and the liability of the guarantor will be no greater than that of the debtor.

The indemnity

A contract of indemnity is a contract between two parties. These are the surety (the indemnifier) who contracts to make good any loss suffered by the creditor (the financier) as a result of a contract which has been entered into with the debtor.

The indemnifier's liability does not solely depend upon the failure of the debtor to pay the sums due, and the indemnifier's liability can be greater than that of the debtor.

The contract of indemnity has two distinct advantages for the creditor. First, sums in excess of the debtor's liability may be secured, and second, the indemnity will not generally be affected by the validity of the principal contract.

The obligation

A contract of guarantee is a primary obligation while a contract of indemnity is a secondary obligation. In other words, the guarantor's obligation depends upon the primary obligation of another party not being discharged. For example, if A says to B 'deliver these items to C and if C does not pay you, then I will', this is a guarantee. And if A says to B 'deliver these items to C and I will make sure you are paid', this is an indemnity.

In deciding between the two, the courts will look to the substance of the transaction as well as the form. Therefore, a contract which makes it clear that the surety is intended to be liable to indemnify the financier against loss, whether or not it is incurred as a result of the lessee's default, is likely to be declared an indemnity.

Amendment of terms

If the creditor and the debtor vary the terms of their agreement without the consent of the surety, the surety will normally be discharged of any responsibilities. This is because the surety is entitled to take over the creditor's rights once the debt has been paid off, but this is not the case if the terms have been altered without the consent of the surety.

These circumstances will include extending the original term, altering the repayment profiles, or the waiver of one or more payments. Most contracts of surety will include a provision that no relaxation, indulgence or variation will affect the surety's liability.

Additional sureties

Liability of more than one surety may be joint, or joint and several. Where the surety is bound jointly with co-sureties, liability for existing and future debts ends on the death of the surety. The creditor may sue one or all of the joint sureties, but the creditor will be unable later to sue those sureties who were missed on the first occasion.

If the sureties are jointly and severally liable, they will each be potentially responsible for the whole of the debt up until the time of any individual's death. Death in itself does not reduce an individual's liability.

Where there is more than one surety, each individual must agree to any amendment to terms otherwise their liability for that transaction will cease.

Subletting agreements

Introduction

Assets which are subject to financial agreements may be let to another party once the financier has indicated agreement. Careful construction of documentation to cover such circumstances is important, otherwise the third party user may establish a right to use the assets for a period of time. When this occurs, the user will be able to continue to use the assets, despite the liquidation or default of the principal creditor, or the termination of the finance contract. Any hire payment received will then be used to apply against the liabilities of the principal creditor generally, and there will be no prior claim by the financier.

Subletting documentation

There are two ways in which the financier can allow the creditor to hire the assets while retaining full rights to them. Both methods assume the creation of an underletting of the assets to the user. The exception will be goods released on very short-term hire, where the financier may be content to await their return at the end of the period. The two methods employed are a registrable assignment and a licensing agreement.

With the registrable agreement, the financier will take an assignment of the underlease as security and will register this interest at Companies House. This has been a common method in 'leverage leasing' where the provider of the funding will be different from the tax shelter provider. While the method has the least legal implications, it has the disadvantages that the creditor will rarely welcome the registration of charges, and the financier will need to take over all responsibilities of the underlease in the event of default by the principal creditor.

With the licensing agreement, a formal licence will be granted to underlet. The licence will contain an acknowledgement for the sublessee. This will state that, in consideration for the grant of the licence to underlet the assets, they will be given up in the event of a default by the principal creditor. This gives the financier a legal right to possession but has the disadvantages that the sublessee will rarely give up the assets voluntarily, and the source of the principal creditor's funding is disclosed.

Most lessors favour the second approach, since they will not then become responsible for maintenance and servicing of the equipment. Special documentation will be needed when the subletting is allowed outside the lessee's own group of companies. Two forms of letter will be required for subletting within a group. These will relate to long-term and short-term subletting.

Long-term licences will confirm the lessor's agreement to the underletting to a specific sublessee. The lessee will acknowledge the responsibility to perform all of the existing obligations of the master lease. The sublessee will be required to substantiate the following items:

1. Capital allowances on the asset could have been claimed by the sublessee had the asset been purchased by the sublessee.
2. The sublessee will comply with the terms of the master lease.
3. The sublessee will give up possession should the lessor demand it.
4. The asset will only be used for the purposes of the sublessee's trade.
5. The sublessee will provide the lessor or any Inspector of Taxes with relevant information when it is required.

Short-term licences will apply when the underletting is created for less than thirty days. This should be established from the terms of the subletting document in order to avoid confusion with fiscal legislation which uses a wider definition. There will be no need to obtain the acknowledgement of the sublessee because of the short-term nature of the contract.

Important points in subletting

The following are some important points to note with subletting:

1. The length of the underlease should always be less than the master lease.
2. The location of the goods is important as this may affect the capital allowances.
3. The insurance cover will need to be reviewed.
4. The formal underlease must not be allowed to conflict with the master lease.
5. The short-term hirings must not exceed defined periods.
6. The underletting could involve the Consumer Credit Act 1974.

The sales agency

In many leasing agreements the lessor will be able to appoint the lessee as the agent to sell the asset at the end of the hiring period. The percentage of the sale proceeds allowed to the lessee will be treated as a refund of rentals, and this percentage will usually be shown in the lease schedule.

The lessor will often not wish to be involved in the sale itself but will want to be satisfied of the following points:

1. The goods are adequately maintained until their disposal.
2. The sale is to a third party so that the capital allowances remain as assumed in the original lease pricing.
3. The liability to the lessor in respect of the asset is minimal.
4. The lessee does not make unauthorised representations concerning the asset on the lessee's own behalf.
5. The lessor is indemnified by the lessee against any liabilities arising from the sale.

Waivers from landlords and debenture holders

In law anything attached to land becomes part of that land. The person owning such an asset is likely to lose ownership of it in favour of the owner of the legal estate in the land.

While it may be the intention of the parties to a lease that the leased assets are not to become fixtures, problems will occur if they are fixed in such a way that damage will be done in the attempt to remove them. In this event they will be deemed to be fixtures.

An agreement will be needed to ensure that the lessor has the right to remove the asset. This agreement will be between the lessee's landlord, or debenture holder, and the lessor. It will be more difficult for the lessor to obtain protection against the claim of mortgagees, or purchasers of the land, whose interest arises after the asset has become fixed. One possible protection might be the registration of the lessor's interest against the title to the land.

Companies and contracts of surety

The authority

The authority of a company to provide contracts of surety will be given in the objects clause of the company's Memorandum of Association. The power to enter into guarantees and indemnities is not implied in law.

The objects clause

An express object in the Memorandum that the company may guarantee the liabilities of others will not include as an object the abilty to enter into contracts of indemnity.

The latest Companies Act (1989) has amended the position relating to the enforceability of a contract which a company has entered into outside the objects of the company. The contract will need to be in the general interest of the company for it to be enforceable against it (i.e. there must be a commercial benefit).

Justifiable relationships

Examples of the type of relationship which might give rise to a commercial justification that a company should become a surety are the following:

- A parent for a subsidiary.
- A subsidiary to a parent.
- Joint venture partners in a trading relationship.
- A buyer to seller or vice versa.
- Inter-company lender to borrower.

The following are not considered to be justifiable relationships:

- Common shareholders or common directors.
- A company to a director.
- A company to an individual.
- A landlord to a tenant.

The terms of a typical corporate guarantee and indemnity

The following are examples of terms of a typical corporate guarantee and indemnity:

1. The financier and the surety will often enter into the agreement although this is not essential.
2. There will be representations by the surety relating its financial standing and its authority to provide a guarantee and indemnity.
3. The guarantor undertakes to pay all amounts payable under the lease, including damages.
4. The guarantor undertakes that the lessee will perform and observe all the obligations under the lease.
5. The surety will agree to pay interest on any amounts unpaid under the guarantee and any legal costs incurred by the lessor in enforcing the guarantee and indemnity.
6. The guarantee obligations will be expressed in a clause in the manner of an indemnity, i.e. they will be payable irrespective of the lessee's liability.
7. The guarantee will often be drawn to catch all schedules made under the leasing agreement.
8. An officer of the lessor shall provide a final and binding statement of the liability to sums due.
9. A clause to set out the actions which may be taken by the lessor under the leasing agreement without prejudice to the surety's liability.
10. A clause to allow the lessor to hold monies paid by the surety on a suspense account without discharging any of the liability under the leasing agreement. This will enable the lessor to prove in bankruptcy as if such monies had not been paid.
11. A clause directed towards allowing the lessor to keep any security given for the surety's liability, in case any payment made by the lessee should be attacked as a fraudulent preference.
12. A clause to postpone the surety's right of subrogation to the lessor's rights until all the lessee's liabilities have been discharged.

13. The surety will be required to agree that the liability under the guarantee and indemnity shall not be affected by any delay on the part of the lessor.
14. Where both parties are UK resident the guarantee will be drawn up under English law. Where foreign parties are involved specialist legal advice will be required.

Contracts with a stated limit

It is common to be offered a guarantee and indemnity valid up to a stated limit. This sum is usually the outstanding rentals at the time of the request. It is often commercially desirable to accept such a proposal. However, the lessor's rights under the guarantee and indemnity will be subrogated to the surety following the surety's payment of the stated liability. The danger exists that the lessor will be unable to enforce against the lessee for any shortfall (or against any other party). Greater complications may arise if there is more than one surety each guaranteeing different amounts.

Letters of comfort

These documents are often offered by parent and holding companies which do not wish to enter into full guarantees and indemnities. They are rarely enforceable since they are not legally binding and have a value of 'moral worth' only.

Summary

There will be many clauses in common within the documentation of asset finance products. The lessor will however take great care to protect the right to capital allowances, and will focus attention on the use to which the asset is put.

Where a secured loan is granted, the financier will be particularly careful to see that the mortgage document is registered correctly within laid down time constraints.

Early settlement

Introduction

Whether the contract is tax-based or not, the financier will have carried out the pricing on the assumption that it is to run for its full term and that the instalments will be paid on the due dates. Where the customer wishes to terminate the contract before the expiry date, the financier will want to be sure to obtain the profit which had been envisaged at the start. There will need to be a mechanism whereby there is provision to deal with early termination within the documentation, and this will need to take tax considerations into account in the case of lease contracts.

Early settlement for leasing

Where the lessee wishes to effect early termination of the lease under the terms of a finance lease, there will be provision for payment of advance rental, or liquidated damages, for breach of contract. The obligation will be calculated by reference to the aggregate of all future rentals which would have become payable had the lease run its full course, together with all arrears of rental.

The lessor will generally agree to discount the future rentals (currently by rates of between 3 and 7 per cent per annum) and, provided the termination has not been effected because of a serious breach of the terms of the lease, to allow the lessee credit for the value of the equipment. The credit will often take the form of a rebate of rentals following the sale of the asset.

Where the lessor is not yet the owner of the asset (since the lessor has funded this acquisition by way of a hire pruchase contract), the credit may be calculated by reference to the market value of the asset at the time of termination.

The approach of the lessor will be constructed so as to avoid any argument that a penalty has arisen from the requirement for a terminal rental equal to the total of outstanding future rentals, since such a penalty may be considered to be void. Even if this were not the case, the lessor would be in the position of making a windfall profit, by being able to lease the asset for the remaining term of the lease, having already effectively received rentals for that period.

The terminal rental will generally be accepted as a trading expense to the lessee and a trading receipt in the hands of the lessor. In the lessee's books of account, the credit will be treated as a refund of rentals.

Where the equipment is sold at the date of termination, the lessor may have made provision to charge a compensating rental should the sale proceeds fail to equal (or exceed) the tax written down value of the asset in order to maintain the post-tax return.

Where the lessee is not in default, the lease documentation will often provide for the lessee to become the agent of the lessor for the purposes of the disposal. The lessee will then be entitled to retain the bulk of the sale proceeds (usually between 90 and 99 per cent), as a refund of rentals.

The general lessor will usually be keen to dispose of the equipment in the most advantageous way, since the lessor's knowledge of a specific market in that equipment is likely to be minimal. Equally, the lessor will not want to take over the responsibilities of such ownership which will revert to the lessor upon the termination of the lease.

The lease will often provide for a rebate of rent so that the lessee will benefit from the insurance proceeds received by the lessor following the total loss, or destruction of the leased asset. After the lessor has taken the terminal sum, the remainder of the proceeds will be passed to the lessee as a rebate.

The payment of a rebate of rentals by the lessor will usually be an acceptable trading expense in the accounting period in which it arises. The amount to be brought into account for capital allowances purposes will be unaffected by the amount of the rebate. For the taxation purposes of the lessee the rental rebate will form a taxable receipt in the hands of the lessee in the year in which it is received.

There is a potential difficulty for the lessee who terminates the lease early on, when few rentals have been paid and the residual value of the leased equipment is still high. When this occurs it is possible for the value of the rebate to exceed the rentals which have been paid. Provided that the lessee treats the rebate as income in the period to which it relates, then it is likely that the Revenue will allow the deduction in respect of the rebate to the lessor. However, the problem could be exacerbated where the lessee is a non-tax paying body.

It is important for the lessor to be seen to acquire capital assets for the purposes of generating an income from the leasing activity. Failure to do so may jeopardise any claim for capital allowances. The lessor will therefore wish to limit the size of the rental rebate on termination in order to demonstrate that a rental stream was generated by the acquisition of the asset.

Early settlement for hire purchase and loan

Early settlement of a loan or a hire purchase agreement will be permitted, and the method used to calculate the sum due from the customer will be determined by whether the agreement falls within the Consumer Credit Act 1974.

Contracts falling within the Consumer Credit Act are known as regulated agreements. Such agreements arise where the customer is an unincorporated body, such as a sole trader or a partnership. Where the customer falls within this category and the balance financed is £15,000, or less, the agreement will be regulated.

The Act stipulates the basis upon which charges are to be rebated upon early settlement by a customer who is not in default of the terms of the agreement. A table of interest rebate will be included in the documentation.

Where the agreement falls outside the Act, the financier will be afforded some flexibility, but it is common to see the settlement calculation for fixed rate agreements based upon the rule of 78 (or sum of digits method as it is sometimes known).

Loan and hire purchase fall into two basic categories, namely fixed rate and linked rate. With fixed rate agreements the customer will receive a settlement figure which will comprise the balance of the capital advanced and interest to the date of settlement and, where appropriate, the option to purchase fee together with any arrears. Interest will generally be calculated by reference to the rule of 78 and may include up to three months' interest, as a charge to compensate the financier for any loss of earnings over the full term of the agreement. The financier will resist too high a charge in case this should be deemed to be a penalty and therefore be considered to be void against the customer. (The rule of 78 will be discussed in detail in Chapter 14.)

With linked rate agreements interest will generally be applied to outstanding balances on a periodic basis at a disclosed margin above an agreed base rate. Upon early settlement, the financier will usually compute the charges until the date of settlement, whence the settlement figure will include the balance of the capital advanced and interest to the date of settlement and, where appropriate, the option to purchase fee together with any arrears. The interest may be 'run on' for up to three months beyond the date of settlement, as a measure to compensate the financier for the breach of the contract. Any additional charge, applied to the customer's account in this way, should be reasonable in relation to the overall contract. If this is not the case, it may be considered to be a penalty with the possibility that the charge may be deemed to be void.

The financier will usually quote a daily rate of charge which will be applied should the customer fail to settle the agreement in full by the agreed date. The customer will be in default of the agreement if the asset subject to the agreement is disposed of prior to full and final settlement being received by the financier.

CHAPTER 8

—————————— ⚱ ——————————

RISK MANAGEMENT

ASSESSING THE RISK

Introduction

Almost all forms of activity involve some element of risk, and the business of asset financing is no exception. For the purposes of the definition of risk within the industry, we refer to the possibility of loss.

There are a number of circumstances in which a financier may incur a loss as a result of business activity, and these revolve around the failure of the customer to make instalments by the due date (if at all). Such failure may be the result of a number of factors, ranging from simple poor financial performance, to the insolvency of the customer, and even to a deliberate fraud.

The assessment of risk can never be considered to be a precise science. The analyst, who interprets the financial information, will be concerned with the past performance of the business in an attempt to predict the future behaviour, and there is no guarantee that the future will mirror the past, even if the economic climate remains the same.

Before entering into the contract, the financier should be satisfied that the customer is:

1. Able to meet the stated repayment profile on the due dates – a test of financial respectability.
2. Willing to meet the stated repayment profile – a test of honesty and reputation.
3. Expected to continue in business throughout the period of the agreement – a test of survival and of stability. In large value transactions the term of the contract may extend to a period in excess of twenty years.

There will be additional, less obvious risks. It should be borne in mind that the financier will enter into a tripartite relationship. The contract will almost always involve a supplier as well as the customer. Generally, the financier will not meet the supplier, the supply of the equipment having been negotiated exclusively by the customer.

Apart from a sales-aid relationship, which is described in Chapter 12, the relationship between the financier and the supplier will be limited to the former settling the latter's invoice to the customer's satisfaction. The financier will need to rely upon the integrity of the supplier to describe the equipment being purchased accurately and honestly. However, there is considerable latitude for fraud within the relationship.

Assessment of the customer

The financier will need to be satisfied that a prospective customer is willing and able to meet the commitments under the terms of the contract, and this will include making payments on the due dates and continuing to trade during the full term of the financial agreement.

The past record of the customer's business will form a reasonable starting point, but the present and future trading prospects will form an increasingly important part of the assessment of the risk involved to the financier as the size of the transaction increases.

The past is best assessed by a thorough examination of, at least, the last three years' audited accounts. The present may be analysed by considering the current activities of the business by reference to its management accounts. The competence of the management may also prove to be a material factor. The future will be investigated from future trading and projected cashflows.

The principles involved in the assessment of the customer will now be looked at in more detail.

The track record

In order to gain a reasonable understanding of a company's progress, it is better to examine the audited accounts over a period of time, and a three year term is generally considered to be the minimum period for effective analysis.

If any period should prove to be in some way exceptional, it will be possible to identify it and ask appropriate questions. An expert accountancy knowledge is not really necessary, but it will be important to recognise the objectives laid down in the published accounts and to be aware of the accounting standards to which they should adhere.

Company accounts

The 1989 Companies Act requires all limited companies to file annual accounts at the Companies Registry. In most cases these will comprise a balance sheet and a profit and loss account. (Companies defined in law as small companies need only file a balance sheet.) All accounts must be audited by a professionally qualified, independent firm of auditors. In addition, to comply with SSAP 10, all companies whose turnover exceeds £25,000 must produce a source and use of funds statement.

The majority of companies will realise that a potential financier will need to have sight of the accounts of the business and will therefore make them available. All companies whose shares are traded on the Stock Exchange must make their published accounts available on request, and indeed many unlisted companies now realise the publicity value in producing informative accounts. The Companies Registry can provide copies of the accounts of a business for a nominal fee.

The profit and loss statement

The profit and loss statement simply shows the results of trading for the financial period for which it is drawn (this will normally be for a period of twelve months – the financial year).

The initial figure will be the turnover. This represents gross sales, after deducting inter-company trading between companies within a group. It comprises all invoices issued to third parties during the financial accounting period. From this figure, all operating and manufacturing costs will be deducted, showing a resultant profit, or loss.

The balance sheet

The balance sheet is a statement of the total assets and the total liabilities of the company on the day it is drawn up. It is a 'snap shop' of the state of affairs of the business on the last day of the financial accounting period. The net assets, after all liabilities have been deducted, should equal the shareholders' funds, i.e. the share capital plus the reserves. The terms 'net assets', 'shareholders' funds' and 'net worth' are all used to describe the 'surplus' retained in a business, and the terms are interchangeable.

The statement of source and application of funds

This statement will show the sources and the applications of funds that come into the business during the financial accounting period. Sources of funds arise from operations, the sale of assets, share issues and borrowings. The application of funds will relate to items such as capital expenditure, payment of dividends, payment of taxes and exceptional items.

Interpretation of the accounts

The profit and loss account and the balance sheet, when compared over a period of time, will provide some indication of the stability and security which the business has to offer the financier. They are products of past performance and will help to build a picture of the business over time.

It is important for the financier to compare trends in a number of areas when assessing the customer's business as a whole. Factors which will prove to be important will include growth in turnover (gross sales), pre-tax profits and the net worth, and it will generally be useful to examine the profit margins which have been achieved over recent years.

The profit margin

Profit margins are calculated by dividing the declared profit by the turnover of the business and multiplying the result by 100 in order to express it as a percentage.

This has the effect of showing how many pence of profit have been achieved in every one pound of sales. A constant, or an increasing profit margin, will usually be quite acceptable, but a falling margin may indicate the onset of future problems and should generally be viewed as a warning sign. Reference can also be made to other businesses within the same market sector, and during the same period, to compare the customer's results with those of similar businesses. This can be a useful exercise in determining its efficiency.

The net worth

Growth in the net worth is of particular importance. This is especially true if it is the result of the issue of additional share capital or from the retention of profits generated, because, in either case, it represents an investment by the shareholders in the future of the company. This will help to instil a degree of confidence in the financier.

Conversely, if a high level of profit were to be distributed to the members, the financier may take a different view, as this may not be in the longer term interests of the company.

Ratio analysis

The simplest way of analysing the balance sheet of a company is by the calculation of a number of significant ratios. The ratios themselves are a reductive device which bring the clumsy figures down to a more manageable proportion.

Liquidity

A company's liquidity should always be considered. This is simply a measurement of the relationship that exists between the current assets – those most easily realised, such as the cash at bank, debtors and stock – and the short-term liabilities, comprising the trade creditors, bank overdraft, etc. Generally, it is best if there is a surplus of these assets over liabilities.

The most basic measurement of liquidity is the current ratio. This is calculated by dividing the current liabilities into the current assets, thus:

$$\frac{\text{Assets}}{\text{Liabilities}} = \frac{£10,000}{£5,000} = 2$$

which is expressed as a ratio of 2:1. The ratio shows that for every £1 of liabilities, there are £2 of assets to cover them. Clearly therefore, the higher this ratio, the better. If the ratio is less than 1:1 this could suggest that future problems are about to develop because the business has insufficient short-term assets to cover the immediate liabilities.

It is important to recognise that the value of this ratio depends upon accurate valuations of the stock and debtors' figures. If some potentially bad debtors are included in the accounts, the integrity of this analysis tool will be lost.

The acid test or quick ratio is a slightly more precise measure of liquidity. This restricts the assets to be used in the calculation to cash and bank balances, trade debtors and quoted investments, all of which should be capable of speedy realisation. It will almost always be lower than the current ratio, and the difference between the two will usually be accounted for by stock. This is because the current ratio effectively looks at the company as a 'going' concern – one that continues trading – whereas the acid test looks at the business as a 'gone' concern – one that is no longer able to trade. In this event, the value of the stock would be negligible.

The gearing ratio is extremely important, as it measures the balance between borrowings and shareholders' funds. The ratio is very easy to calculate and it includes all borrowings (both long and short term, including bank overdrafts, loans, finance leasing and lease purchase liabilities, mortgages, etc.), the total of which is divided by the total of the shareholders' funds (the net worth). The latter will comprise the total of the issued share capital, together with all reserves, less any intangible assets, such as goodwill.

There is no such thing as an ideal gearing ratio, but it should be borne in mind that if it were 1:1, then the borrowings and the net worth are the same which will rarely be viewed as a particularly desirable state of affairs for a UK company. As a general rule, the lower the ratio the better, but it will always be necessary to consider the gearing in context. Some industries, by their nature, will be more prone to heavy borrowings than others.

For example, a supermarket, which is primarily a cash generating business, would not usually need to borrow extensively, and will therefore have a gearing ratio of well below 1:1. Conversely, a business which is involved in substantial research, development or exploration costs, such as many companies in the oil industry, may need to borrow in anticipation of future earnings.

Both the financier and the customer should recognise that the new facility will normally add to the company's borrowings, unless it is truly of a replacement nature. As such, it should be included in the gearing calculation.

Interest cover

It can be argued that the size of a company's borrowings only represent part of the picture, and it will be important to consider how the company will service the payment of interest. Interest cover should therefore be assessed.

The amount of interest which accrues in any one accounting period will always be shown in the accounts for that period, as will the profit before interest and tax (sometimes referred to as the operating profit). The number of times which the interest figure can be divided into the profit before interest and tax figure will demonstrate how many times the profit generated could have covered the interest bill. Unequivocally, the higher the number of times, the better the result will appear.

A low figure, generally less than three times the cover, indicates that the business should be cautious regarding future borrowings which could prove to be sensitive to adverse movements in interest rates.

Working capital

A company cannot exist without working capital. Its funds will be tied up in stock and in debtors (the money owed to it by its customers) and will be offset by the money which it owes to its creditors. There are various measurements which can be used to assess a company's efficiency at managing its working capital.

It is important to know how long the average debtor takes to pay the invoice (debtor days), and this is calculated by dividing the trade debtors' figure shown in the balance sheet by the turnover (the gross sales) in the profit and loss account, and then multiplying the result by 365, thus:

$$\frac{\text{Trade debtors}}{\text{Turnover}} \times 365$$

If the accounts are drawn up for other than a period of a year, the figure of 365 will require adjustment. The result shows the average number of debtor days. This can be measured more precisely by averaging the debtor's figure, then adding together the trade debtors' figure shown for the most recent year and the same figure for the previous year, and then dividing the result by two.

This should be judged in context. In the case of a supermarket, which rarely gives trade credit, the result should be very low, whereas other industries, such as those with major exports, may often be seen to have long debtor periods. Generally, the shorter the period the better, as this will tend to imply good control.

The approach to the number of days of credit taken by the business (creditor days) will be similar. The trade creditors in the balance sheet will be divided by the cost of sales figure extracted from the profit and loss account, and the result multiplied by 365. An averaging process can also be carried out. The result will provide an indication of how long the company takes to pay its suppliers.

If this period is significantly shorter than the debtors' period, it may reflect poor financial management. If, on the other hand, payment appears to be slow, it may be indicative of a strain on cash resources.

Stock turnover can be an important ratio, and it is derived simply by dividing the stock figure from the balance sheet into the turnover. It provides an indication of the number of times the stock moves in a year. The supermarket may be expected to turn over most of its stock, many times in a year, whereas an engineering concern may only turn its stock two or three times during a comparable period.

Context and commercial attitude are vitally important in the interpretation of this type of financial analysis.

The present

Where the financier's representative has visited the prospective customer, a comprehensive report will be produced, which will be vital to the assessment process. This report should contain answers to the following questions:

- What are the main areas of activity of the business?
- Are these planned to change during the term of the financial agreement, and if so, what is the impact likely to be upon the business as a whole?
- What products are manufactured or distributed?
- What level of demand for products is foreseen in the future?
- Does the business rely upon raw materials that are scarce or which are supplied from politically sensitive areas?
- Who are the major suppliers and how many are there in the market?
- Who are the major customers?
- Does the business rely upon a few major customers within a single industry sector? (Generally, a company which has a limited spread of customers will be more vulnerable than one with a large number of customers operating in a variety of industries).
- Are there forward contracts with customers or does the business simply rely on repeat orders?
- Who are the senior managers; what are their qualifications and experience, and what other business interests do they have?

Management figures

Due to the time taken for their preparation, the audited accounts will already be somewhat out of date by the time they are published. As part of the examination of the customer's present trading, the prudent financier will be well advised to request information regarding the up-to-date management accounts. These are accounts which are prepared internally to enable the company's management to monitor its progress on a regular basis. They will not be audited, and they will frequently be drawn up in a different format to the audited results. However, these figures can be a most useful adjunct to the formal audited accounts, but the financier will need to be satisfied as to their accuracy and completeness.

It is not uncommon for the company's management to be unwilling to release management accounts, arguing that they are confidential documents. Further, in the case of quoted companies whose shares are listed on the Stock Exchange, there will be the added risk of 'insider trading' if their content became public. It is however extremely difficult for the financier to conduct a thorough credit, or risk, analysis without some access to management accounting information, and even a verbal indication on the present trading progress will be preferable to none at all.

The analysis of management accounts should be as thorough as possible in order to identify any significant trends. If there are seen to be any significant divergences from past results, these should be investigated, even if, on the face of it, the movement favours the business.

If there is a balance sheet, the ratios already discussed should be calculated, although it will often be necessary to allow for seasonal variations, and possibly even alternative accounting policies. It is of note that the majority of businesses select the date for the end of their financial year to show the company in the best possible light.

For example, if the management accounts of an ice cream manufacturer were to be examined in June and then again at the end of December, there would be significant differences in the debtor days, the turnover and the gearing ratio. The turnover and profit figures are likely to be greater during the summer months than in the winter, and it will be important to reflect the seasonal nature of the trade in order to avoid the possibility of projecting inaccurate future cashflows.

The future

The financier will need to feel comfortable that the customer will survive during the period of the financial contract and be able to meet the instalments when they fall due for payment. The stability of the business can be assessed effectively by reference to the past and present, but to assess the ability to meet future instalments, some reference should be made to the cashflow statements.

The internal cashflow

Basically this is represented by the pre-tax profits generated by the business, less any extraordinary items, plus depreciation charged during the period. From this the company has to provide for its working capital and its capital expenditure, pay its taxes and dividends and make any contracted loan repayments. Lease rentals will also be met from the cashflow. If the internal cashflow is insufficient, additional borrowing, either by way of overdraft or loan, will be required, unless the company is able to persuade its members to subscribe for additional shares in the business.

The source and application of funds statement will show these, among other, items. The sources of funds will include the pre-tax profit, depreciation, the proceeds arising from the sale of fixed assets and from the issue of any new shares. The uses of funds will generally include capital expenditure, payment of taxes and dividends and any capital repayment of loans. The statement will also show the working capital position.

If the company's internal cashflow is persistently insufficient to fund the working capital requirements of the business, this may imply a weakness on the part of the management. It may be that invoices are not being paid quickly enough, or that stock control is weak. It may even be that invoices are being settled too quickly, but something will certainly be wrong with the level of financial control and the financier should be wary.

Ideally, a company should be able to meet its working capital needs and make tax and dividend payments from the internal cashflow, without resort to further borrowing. It is difficult to arrive at meaningful analysis of future cashflows, at least without access to the internal projections. However, it should be possible, at least in part, to project the future cash outflows by careful study of the notes contained within the published accounts. For example, the notes will contain a breakdown of all future loan repayments, split into short term (due within the following twelve months), medium term (due within one to five years), and long term (those due after five years). Since the acceptance of SSAP 21 with regard to lease accounting, the rentals in respect of finance and operating leases will generally be treated in a similar manner.

There will usually be notes in respect of future capital commitments, stating whether these have simply been authorised or whether they are, indeed, contracted, but not provided for in the accounts.

It is possible to construct a grid on which to record this information as follows:

	Next year	1–5 years	Over 5 years
Loan repayments			
Finance lease rentals			
Operating lease rentals			
Property lease rentals			
Contracted commitments	_____	_____	_____
Total outflows	_____	_____	_____

Having assessed these anticipated outflows, the analyst can then attempt to decide whether the past internal cashflows have been sufficient to cover them. It will, however, be important to recognise that no provision has been made for tax, dividends, replacement capital expenditure or working capital.

Projections

The majority of prudent companies will forecast their results for at least the current financial year. Their management will use the management accounts as a tool to monitor progress against these forecasts, or projections. Where the customer has been willing to release the management accounts, there may also be a willingness to release the projections.

While the projections will doubtless be completed with a high degree of accuracy, the financier should view them with caution. If a company forecasts a sudden increase in its profitability, or perhaps a recovery from a loss making period, it should question how such an improvement is going to be achieved.

Should there be a prediction of a large increase in sales, the financier should enquire whether there has been adequate provision for the necessary increase in working capital. Where it has, how is it to be funded? Can it be funded internally or will some additional external borrowing be required? Will an increased funding cost impact on the forecast profit and has due provision been made? Are the forecast results in line with the performance of similar companies in the same industry, and in tune with the economy as a whole?

If both the projections and the management accounts have been drawn up on a month-by-month, or a quarter-by-quarter basis, then it will be possible to verify the actual results with the forecasted results. Clearly, if the actual performance varies significantly from that forecast, the value of future projections will be brought into question.

It is vital that the financier is satisfied with the potential for future trading since receiving the repayments will depend upon the realisation of the future success.

Credit reference agencies

In the foregoing, we have been addressing the fact that the financier will need to be satisfied that the customer is both able to meet the payment dates on which instalments will be due and capable of surviving throughout the term of the contract. We have not yet discussed the question of the customer being willing to meet the instalments. This will, essentially, be a question of corporate integrity.

There will never be a substitute for a relationship with an existing customer, from which an established track record has been built up over a period of time. However, the relationship has to start somewhere, and the financier may often find it beneficial to consult a credit reference agency, prior to accepting business from a new customer. This can be particularly valuable in the small ticket and sales-aid markets, where up-to-date accounts may be unavailable and the opportunity for detailed discussion is limited.

There are several agencies of this type in the United Kingdom, but the two who have been established the longest are Infolink (formerly The United Association for the Protection of Trade) and Dun and Bradstreet. The information from both will generally be of a similar quality. However, Dun and Bradstreet restricts its reporting service to limited liability companies, whereas Infolink can also report on sole traders and partnerships. The service is available from both either in paper copy or over dedicated telephone lines.

The reports are provided on a fee-paying basis and the financier may select the length of the report and the detail contained in it. The report can include the following:

- A confirmation of the registered name and the trading style.
- A confirmation of the registered office address.
- Details of any parent, subsidiary, or associated companies.
- Details of the directors.
- Details of any judgments registered against the company in the County Courts.
- Trade and supplier references.

Additionally, both agencies are willing to provide copies of the information filed at the Companies Registry, and this can include the most recently filed accounts.

Interpretation of information

Generally, the financier will be cautious of being exposed to risk by the provision of facilities to a business against which there have been recent judgments in the County Courts.

To the financier, there may often be less relevance to the trade and supplier references, since many business people take a different view to finance commitments than they do to supplier credit. For example, exceeding the trade terms afforded by a supplier of stationery is unlikely to have the same consequences as missing repayments to a financier.

The reports from a credit reference agency can be useful for background information, but are unlikely to prove sufficient for the financier to reach a positive decision without some additional information, unless the transaction is very modest in size.

Assessment of the supplier

For an instalment credit transaction to offer a high degree of security to the financier, the integrity of the supplier will become an important issue. Despite this, it remains rare for the financier to meet the supplier, all arrangements being concluded between the supplier and the customer. Notwithstanding this, the financier will acquire title to the asset and settle the supplier's invoice.

A further complication arises by virtue of the fact that the financier will rarely see the asset at any point during the buying process. In effect, the financier will therefore rely upon the good faith of the supplier and the customer for confirmation that the asset even exists at all. In the sales-aid market, these risks are considerably reduced because of the relationship which exists between the financier and the introductory source, but in other circumstances the financier will always bear a certain degree of risk.

The financier who specialises in a specific market sector will soon get to know the major equipment suppliers and the equipment which they finance, but the general practitioner, willing to handle a wide range of assets, will encounter more problems. Careful vetting of the customer, and possibly the establishment of a register of approved suppliers, will afford some degree of protection, and some companies hold a database of suppliers from whom they will automatically accept invoices for approved transactions.

The information which they maintain in these databases will generally include the following:

- The name and address of the supplier.
- The types of assets handled.
- Details of agencies and franchises.
- The number and size of previous transactions.
- Where this occurs, the register will be checked at the same time that the credit request is received. Occasionally a report on a new supplier may be obtained from one of the credit reference agencies.

Fraud

It is extremely difficult for the financier to be protected from the attentions of the professional fraudster. Fraud can arise as a result of the actions of the customer or the supplier alone, but more commonly the customer and the supplier will work together to perpetrate the deception. Fraud can take several forms, but the most common are multiple financing, non-existent equipment, inflated cost and connected companies.

Multiple financing refers to where the same item of equipment is financed from several sources. In these cases, more than one invoice will be generated in respect of the same asset. This will result in several financiers believing that they have acquired good title.

This is probably the most difficult fraud to detect, because each financier will receive what appears to be an original supplier's invoice. Occasionally the fraudster will make an error, such as omitting the VAT number, but most are very professional, even establishing a temporary base at the address described in case the financier should choose to call the telephone number on the invoice for confirmation.

There is also fraud where an invoice will be issued for a non-existent asset. This is equally difficult to detect, but stringent checks on invoices may have some effect. For example, invoices which offer only vague descriptions, such as 'machinery', or 'computer equipment', should not be accepted. Professional invoices will have a full product description, together with serial numbers, and can be invaluable should the equipment have to be repossessed at a later date, since they will assist considerably in the process of identification.

Inflation of the value of an asset is the most common form of fraud in the second-hand market. In the case of new equipment, it is useful to obtain a manufacturer's brochure and price list, where the financier has limited knowledge of a specialist piece of plant. This will assist in identification of the asset should this be necessary and verify the value charged on the invoice.

Where the equipment is second hand, the financier will be well advised to ascertain its age, its present and anticipated working life, and its original cost. An independent valuation with regard to the invoiced price can usually be obtained from a valuer, and sometimes from the original manufacturer. The second-hand value of hightech equipment can vary tremendously and a close inspection by the financier would be beneficial.

Where the supplier and the customer are connected by common shareholders, the financier should take special care. The financier should be satisfied that the equipment exists, is as it is described, that the price is reasonable and that the financier obtains a satisfactory title.

Assessing the suitability of the asset

The financier will generally rely upon the asset to realise the balance of the investment should the customer fail to honour the terms of their agreement. Therefore, the financier may need to recover the asset at some later date in which case the asset should be capable of identification.

In the case of items such as vehicles, identification should rarely be a problem. However, where the equipment is of a more specialist nature, identification can become a complex issue. There will be no substitute for completeness, both in the description on the invoice (a copy of which should physically be attached to the schedule to the contract) and in the schedule itself.

The financier will be well advised to consider the future value of the asset for which finance is sought against the type of use to which his customer will put it. Upon repossession, some assets will have held their value far better than others, because there is an established second user market for them.

Generally speaking, except in periods of severe recession, vehicles, constructors' plant and printing equipment have a reasonably stable depreciation pattern. Manufacturing equipment depreciation rates tend to vary with their application and their degree of sophistication. Ships and aircraft can be problematic, while many small computers lose their value very quickly.

The following assets often cause problems to the financier who is forced to dispose of them but the list is by no means exhaustive:

- Computers,
- Furnishings,
- Sewing machines,
- Typewriters,
- Photocopiers,
- Carpets,
- Word processors,
- Facsimile machines.

Making the decision

Risk assessment is not a precise science. There is no universal set of rules. However, it is possible to provide some general pointers as follows:

1. The customer's track record should have demonstrated the ability and the integrity to meet the future instalments on the due dates.
2. The financier should be satisfied that the customer is solvent and will survive the term of the contract which has been proposed.
3. The description of the asset should be complete and allow for the ready identification of the equipment should this be necessary.
4. The value of the asset should not exceed the value of the company – in other words, the new financial contract should not be of such a size that it will grossly distort the gearing of the business as a whole.
5. Wherever possible, the financier should attempt to structure the portfolio of facilities to match the financier's own underlying borrowing. It may seem a good idea to link to fluctuating money costs when rates are high, in the hope of taking a windfall profit when rates fall. However, this is a dangerous way for the financier to fund the lending book, particularly where it contains substantially all fixed rate contracts with customers.

   There will be no guarantee that market rates will fall when they are predicted to do so. For the financier whose only profit will arise from the return on funds employed within the contract, there is unlikely to be sufficient margin to withstand an upward movement in the cost of funds.

   The financier's lending book will need to be balanced to avoid the need to refresh a large part of the borrowings at one time. In so doing, the financier will substantially reduce the risks which accompany the fluctuations in the money markets, by spreading the period over which it will be necessary to seek further funds.
6. The smaller financier should generally restrict the maximum amount to be provided to one customer or one transaction. In this way, losses will be limited if the customer or the contract fail. The financier will often be able to seek a fee for the introduction of a large transaction from another financier.
7. The lessor will need to provide for the effects of taxation in the leasing contracts. The lessor should carefully monitor the capacity to write leasing business and maintain a close watch on the structure of individual transactions. In this way the lessor is likely to be able to benefit from the fiscal benefits which will accrue to the owner of the leased asset, without the risk of a refusal by the Inland Revenue.

Summary

The financier will have many areas of potential risk and the support systems which are developed by the financier will need to take account of all the factors which can impact upon the business. Management and staff should be given clear limits to their authority.

REDUCING THE RISK

Introduction

The financier will want to minimise the possibility of loss at the start of the contract with a customer. No amount of security can turn a bad deal into a good deal, only into a less bad one. Risk is, as has been suggested earlier, by no means a precise science, and the definitions of acceptable and unacceptable transactions will vary from financier to financier. Even within the same organisation, policy will change from time to time to reflect the state of the marketplace. There will therefore be some occasions where transactions may not stand up by themselves, but, with additional security, they will nevertheless be acceptable.

It is sometimes argued that, as the financier is the owner of the asset under the terms of a leasing or hire purchase agreement, the title to the asset is, in itself, a form of security. There is a degree of truth in this: many organisations might accept a less creditworthy transaction if the equipment comprised, for example, a vehicle fleet, but not if they were asked to fund office furniture.

Generally, though, financiers will seek some way of reducing the risk inherent in the less creditworthy transaction. This could take the form of reducing the period, or increasing the value of the first instalment to be paid by the customer. Much of the time, however, additional security will be sought. This additional security can take several forms and these include guarantees and indemnities, letters of comfort and debentures. (Guarantees and debentures are discussed below; letters of comfort are discussed on page 101; and debentures are discussed on page 102.)

Guarantees and indemnities

A guarantee is a promise made by the guarantor to answer for the present or future debts of the customer (the principal debtor). The promise is made to the creditor (the financier) to whom the customer is, or will become, liable. A guarantee creates a contingent liability. Liability remains with the principal debtor and the guarantor (the surety) only becomes liable if and when the principal debtor fails to perform the obligations under the principal contract (the financing agreement). The contract must be in writing and the liability of the guarantor cannot exceed that of the principal debtor.

An indemnity is a contract between two parties, the creditor and the surety (the indemnifier), with the latter promising to make good any loss suffered by the creditor as a result of a contract between the creditor and the debtor.

The financier will generally attempt to perfect the security as both a guarantee and an indemnity. The difference between the two is often misunderstood, but it is essentially as follows. If the principal debtor fails to fulfil the terms of the original contract, the creditor, under a guarantee, must first take action against the debtor before pursuing the guarantor. Under the terms of an indemnity the creditor may pursue the indemnifier without first pursuing the debtor.

The benefit of writing the security in terms of both an indemnity and a guarantee will arise from the fact that the financier has available a choice of two courses of action, with the greater probability of settlement of the debt because of the speed with which he will be able to act.

Assessing the security

The financier should always wish to be sure that the customer (principal debtor) is capable of fulfilling the contract without the need of additional security. Where it is considered prudent to seek the comfort of additional security, perhaps for reasons based on the short length of time that the business has been established, or the size of the transaction in relation to the overall worth of the customer's business, the financier would be wise to assess the ability of the surety to fulfil the contract if called upon to do so. In other words, just as the financier must be certain that the customer can and will meet the rentals when they fall due, and will survive the period of the contract, the financier should also be certain that the surety, too, can and will meet the payments and will survive.

Where the surety offered is a limited company, it can be assessed in the same manner as described in the earlier part of this chapter. Indeed, where a parent company is being assessed in respect of a guarantee for one or more of its subsidiary companies, the main point of reference will be the group, or consolidated, accounts. (It should be noted that the parent alone should also be assessed, as far as possible, as it will often be the case that its only tangible assets are the shares it owns in its subsidiaries. If those subsidiaries were to fail, then its shares would be worthless.)

Where individuals – for example, company directors – offer their personal guarantees, the financier should attempt to ascertain the extent of their personal assets. In many cases it may transpire that, apart from their private houses (which will usually be subject to at least one mortgage), their main assets will be their shareholdings in their company. If the company failed, their shares would have little or no value. It should be acknowledged that guarantees given by the directors of the company will often be more of a symbolic than a tangible value, and indicate their faith in the future of their company.

The reports from credit reference agencies can prove to be very useful aids in assessing the integrity of personal sureties. It should be noted that there is no accurate way of confirming the extent of the contingent liability of an individual under personal guarantees. In the case of a limited company, information will be provided as a note to the accounts. The financier must assess whether the full facts are available at the point of underwriting the transaction.

Commercial benefit

It is sometimes assumed that all *intra vires* guarantees given by limited companies will be equally enforceable, but the question of commercial benefit should be considered by the financier. The complexities of this subject are beyond the scope of a general work of this nature, but it may be taken as a general concept that companies should not engage in activities that do not give them some benefit.

Guarantees can be divided into the following three categories:

1. Downstream.
2. Upstream.
3. Cross-stream.

An example of a downstream guarantee would be from a parent company to a subsidiary, and as the parent can be assumed to benefit from the activity of the subsidiary, commercial benefit can be assumed to exist.

An upstream guarantee would occur where the subsidiary company guarantees its parent. Here proof of benefit will be more difficult. However, as most subsidiaries receive some service from their parent, it can be argued that it will be to their benefit for the parent to continue trading.

The area of the cross-stream guarantee is the most difficult. One example of such a guarantee would be where one subsidiary company guarantees a fellow subsidiary without the parent being involved. Another example would arise where a company provided a guarantee in respect of a completely separate company. In both circumstances there will need to be a definite trading relationship between the two companies that will be affected in some way by the transaction that is being guaranteed. For instance, if company A was the sole manufacturer, or supplier, of a product used by company B and was about to enter into a new contract with company B for an increased supply, a lease for a new machine to be used by company A solely to fulfil the contract could be guaranteed by company B. In this case, company B would derive benefit by virtue of its commercial relationship with company A.

The financier should always consider the question of commercial benefit so as to be successful in collecting payment as a result of that security.

Release and determination

A surety may give notice that it wishes to determine its liability, and, if that is permitted by the guarantee itself, the practical effect will be that the surety's liability will be restricted to the sum outstanding under the principal contract at the time of determination. There will often be a period of notice before determination is possible.

The financier should bear in mind that any further advances to, or contracts with, the principal debtor will not be covered by the guarantee, and therefore any further credit requirements should be reassessed.

There is generally no obligation on a financier to release a surety from its guarantee. Such a request will be judged on its merits, and will doubtless involve further credit assessment of the principal debtor, and, possibly reflection on commercial, market forces also wishing to secure the business.

Amendment of terms

The financier should be mindful that any amendment to the terms of the principal contract – for example, a moratorium on payments, or a change to the repayment profile – must have the consent of the surety, otherwise the surety is effectively released from its obligations.

Letters of comfort

Letters of comfort, or letters of awareness, are sometimes offered as substitutes for parent company guarantees in respect of facilities granted to subsidiary companies. Such letters will be addressed to the financier and signed on behalf of the parent company. While there is no set format for their content, they will usually state that the company is a subsidiary, and that the parent is aware of the facility which is being provided by the financier. Some letters will additionally state that the parent will use its best endeavours to see that its subsidiary fulfils its obligations, or that the financier will not incur a loss by granting the facilities.

The important point from the financier's point of view is that they have no legal force whatsoever. At best they create a moral obligation and should therefore be reserved for organisations of the hightest integrity only.

GIVING AND TAKING SECURITY

Introduction

A trading company can borrow money, give security and enter into leases without a specific provision in the Memorandum and Articles. Any company can mortgage its partly paid-up shares for the balance remaining unpaid. However, the owners of a business may prefer not to give formal security beyond title to the asset during the currency of the agreement with the financier. This will often influence the type of finance product chosen. Serious thought should always be given to the question of providing additional security, as this could possibly limit future borrowing opportunities with other lenders.

Most banks will require security against an advance for the acquisition of plant and equipment, as ownership of those assets will be vested in the customer and not the bank. Other financiers and lessors may be content to rely on the asset value, if the user is providing some degree of advance payment at the start of the contract and the asset has a slow rate of depreciation. Where security is provided, it can take several forms.

Debenture issues

Additional capital can be raised by debenture issue. The debenture is a document given by the company to the debenture holder, as evidence of a mortgage or charge on the assets of the company, in return for a loan on interest. The debenture holder becomes a creditor of the company, and often holds one of a series of debentures each with similar rights attached to them.

Most debentures will be contained in a formal trust deed, giving a charge over fixed assets and a floating charge over the remaining assets of the company.

Floating charges

A floating charge, allowing the company to deal freely with business assets, will not be available to the sole trader or partnership. Companies will be able to create separate fixed and floating charges. A floating charge will always be enforceable after a fixed charge, in whichever order they were made, unless the floating charge prohibits a loan with prior rights on the security of the fixed assets and the lender under the fixed charge is aware of the restriction.

Problems arising on winding up

Difficulties will often occur for the borrower who has run into a liquidity problem. If a company is forced out of business for this reason, a floating charge created within six months of winding up will be invalid unless the company was solvent when the charge was created.

Debentures may also be invalidated if they were made in favour of individual creditors within six months of the winding up. This might apply if the debentures were created in order to reduce the liability of a director under a personal guarantee. Repayment will then be postponed to the rights of preferred and secured creditors, and in some cases the directors may have to repay the lender themselves.

Registration of charges

Under the 1989 Companies Act, all charges on any property are registrable. If a debenture or loan is secured on assets, the charge will be fixed. A charge over all the company's assets is a floating charge, as the security changes from time to time. A floating charge will automatically crystallise into a fixed charge when the company is wound up or its trading ceases. This will also apply when the company falls into default under the terms of the loan, and the debenture holder proceeds to enforce the security.

Specific particulars will be sent to the Registrar of Companies within twenty-one days of their creation and can be lodged by anyone interested in the charge. Charges not registered will be void against administrators, liquidators and purchasers for value of the property charged. The creditor will be unable to enforce the security unless the time for registration is extended by the courts. If any of the particulars are inaccurate, the charge will only be void to the extent of the inaccuracy, unless the courts order otherwise.

Both the company and its officers can be fined for non-registration, and late or further particulars can now be registered. Late particulars validate the charge, unless the company has become insolvent in the interim, or will become insolvent if the charge is enforced and insolvency proceedings commenced within the 'relevant period'. The 'relevant period' for floating charges will be calculated from the date of registration, and will run for two years if the creditor is a connected person and one year if an outsider. The 'relevant period' for other charges will be for six months.

To remove a charge, a memorandum of satisfaction signed by both the chargee and the chargor must be forwarded to the Registrar.

Effect of the 1989 Companies Act

From March 1991, the following charges must be registered:

1. Charges on land, but not a rent charge.
2. Charges on goods (including ships and aircraft) unless the chargee is entitled to possession of the goods or of the document of title.
3. Charges on intangible moveable property, such as goodwill, intellectual property and book debts (both on the company's book debts and on debts assigned to the company).
4. Uncalled share capital and calls made but unpaid.
5. Charges for securing a debenture issue.
6. Floating charges on company property.
7. Floating charges over shares and other securities do not require registration but the rights attached to them (e.g. dividend payments) may make it advisable to attempt to register them.
8. Charges over property abroad must be registered, and a retention of title clause may be a deemed book debt and therefore registrable.

A bank's charge on credit balances will not be registrable unless charged to a third party, and a charge over 'book debts and other debts' does not include a credit balance with the company's bank.

Charges on registered land must be registered under the Land Registration Act 1925 and fixed charges on unregistered land registered under the Land Charges Act 1972.

Company register

The company must keep a register of charges, available for public inspection at its registered office. Copies of instruments creating charges must be kept at the registered office and be available for inspection by creditors and shareholders.

Selecting the security to be given

It will often be in the interest of the company, when looking at ways to finance its fixed assets, to consider alternative sources of funds from financiers, who will be prepared to accept the asset as the principal security for the funds advanced.

Often finance companies will be prepared to negotiate facilities without the requirements to register charges. This will have the benefit to the customer that the other assets in the business remain unencumbered and therefore available as security for working capital requirements.

CHAPTER 9

✝

LEASE VERSUS PURCHASE
CONSIDERATIONS

Introduction

Tables have been published which show the effective before-tax interest rates of rentals over a range of primary periods with various payment intervals. These tables demonstrate how the rental payment may be expressed as if it were the repayment for a loan at interest. The rental payment shown in this way will be less than a loan payment relating to the same initial amount, in view of the consequence of tax relief in the form of capital allowances.

The difference between this effective rate of a rental stream and the rate of interest on a loan on equivalent terms is a suitable measure for the non-tax paying organisation, provided that the compounding period applied to the interest is the same for both types of product. The comparison will demonstrate the cost advantage (or otherwise) of leasing to such a body.

However, for a tax paying company a more detailed analysis would be necessary before committing to some major expenditure, because of the impact of capital allowances available to the owner of the asset. As the cashflows from one finance source are likely to be of different amounts, and occur at different levels, to an alternative source, a method of analysis will be required which can take account of the time value of money, by discounting future cashflows to the present time at a given interest rate.

Discounted cashflow methods

The two most common discounted cashflow methods are the internal rate of return, and the net present value. There is a third method, known as the annual capital charge method which is used by some nationalised bodies and others who use a sinking fund basis to charge depreciation. This method compares the average annual charge for depreciation and interest with the annual net cashflows, but is not now commonly used in the evaluation of lease rental costs.

The internal rate of return method finds the discount rate which discounts the future cashflows to the same amount as the initial cash outlay. This rate is then compared with the chosen discount rate to evaluate the attractiveness of the project. Essentially, each rental is appreciated to have an element of capital and interest within it. Once the interest element is removed (the discount rate) the rentals, now comprising only the capital element, will equal the initial investment.

The net present value method discounts future cashflows back to the start date of the project using a predetermined discount rate. This discounted value is then compared with the initial investment which gave rise to the cashflows. In other words, each cashflow is reduced by the chosen discount rate, and then each discounted cashflow value is added to the next in order to arrive at the total of all cashflows. The total of the discounted cashflows can finally be compared with the initial outlay of the project.

Discount methods in lease rental evaluation

Either of the discounted cashflow methods can be used to evaluate the lease rentals, and there are a number of preprogrammed financial calculators (such as the Hewlett Packard 12C), which are of great assistance in the investigation of discounted cashflows.

Before attempting any detailed analysis, it is important to be aware of the potential pitfalls which can arise, when, for instance the net cashflow changes from positive to negative, or vice versa. When this happens, multiple internal rate solutions are possible, and for the sake of clarity, this is illustrated by Example 9.1.

It is possible to resolve this potential problem (illustrated in Example 9.1) by using the dual rate of return method (sometimes known as the extended yield method). To do this it is initially necessary to identify all periods in which the cumulative cashflows produce a cash surplus, when discounted at the internal rate of return. These cashflows are then discounted at a predetermined rate (the rate required from the project), in order to calculate the internal rate of the remaining cashflows. This is a particularly important technique when conducting the evaluation of a project which has surplus cash generated during a part of its term.

It should be recognised that, in the net present value method, an assumption has to be made, that the funds returned by the initial investment can be reinvested at the same rate of interest as that used to discount the

---

Example 9.1 Changes of cashflow from positive to negative, and vice versa

An initial investment of £3,950 generates the following cashflows in the next three years:

	£
Year 0	−3,950
Year 1	+13,102
Year 2	−14,500
Year 3	+5,350
	+ 2

The overall return on the initial investment is £2, hardly a significant contribution on the face of it. However, the cashflows do satisfy an internal rate of return of 5 percent, 10 percent and 15 percent as follows:

Year	Cash £	5% £	10% £	15% £
1	13,102	12,476	11,909	11,391
2	(14,500)	(13,152)	(11,984)	(10,964)
3	5,350	4,622	4,020	3,518
	3,952	3,946	3,945	3,945

The problem of multiple internal rate solutions which can confuse the decision maker can arise when the cashflow is positive during one period and negative during another. Every change of sign gives rise to an additional solution.

---

cashflow. If the discount rate is equal to the rate at which the firm is able to borrow capital over a similar term, this should be acceptable, provided that the results of the project do not mean that the business finds its financial position changing from that of a net borrower to a temporary surplus of cash, with the consequent analysis considerations which that involves.

The choice of appropriate methods

It is generally accepted that the net present value (NPV) method of discounting cashflow is easier to understand than the internal rate of return (IRR) method. This is principally because it avoids the problems arising from multiple rate solutions and discounting surplus funds at a yield rate. NPV can also cope with multiple discount rates over a period of time.

Conversely, IRR can often provide a more useful measure of profitability when assessing risk projects, and it does not need to apply the cost of capital of the business, if this has yet to be resolved.

Some basic principles

There are a few basic principles which should be essential to every transaction when discounted cashflow methods are employed. These are as follows:

1. Due regard should be paid to the financial structure and taxation position of an individual business at the point of the proposed investment.
2. All of the receipts and payments, including taxation, should be accounted for on a net of tax basis in order to ensure that timing differences are fully reflected.
3. While all calculations need to be predicted accurately, assumptions should be simplified wherever possible.
4. It should be borne in mind that a relatively tiny adjustment to the discount rate could make a significant difference to the present value, and therefore the discount rate used should be carefully selected.

The procedure

The net present value method relies upon the comparison of the present value of the lease cashflows with the initial cost of the asset subject to the leasing contract, less the present value of the tax relief granted. If the discount rate chosen is the rate that the business would pay on a loan of equivalent amount over a similar term, there is no need to evaluate the firm's borrowing cashflows. This is because discounting at the inherent interest rate (or internal rate of return), only, has the effect of eliminating the interest cost with the result that the present value of the cashflows is equal to the initial amount of the advance.

Choosing the most appropriate rate

This is the most difficult area of discounted cashflow analysis. Lease evaluation is generally treated as a separate area and this, at least, avoids the need to use a discount rate calculated in a manner that reflects the weighted average of the cost of capital of the business.

Practical difficulties will inevitably arise in deciding upon the appropriate borrowing discount rate, including the following:

1. The fact that borrowing rates for an equivalent capital sum will often vary year on year. Yields on government securities vary according to the date of their maturity and structured loans, wherein rates increase in later years, are available. It is possible to avoid the need for different discount rates by selecting a middle rate but the calculations are likely to be distorted when the borrowing yield curve is steep.

2. The structure of comparative cashflows will be different because of the impact of tax relief received on the lease rental payments.

3. The discount rate may need to be adjusted to reflect the different compounding periods employed in the loan contract.

4. Where the decision is between using surplus cash or leasing, the discount rate should reflect the earnings opportunity of the respective funds (the opportunity cost) and not the cost of borrowing. A suitable rate may be the average rate which may be gained from the average yield on government securities maturing over the lease period, or an equivalent deposit in the inter-bank market. Both this earning opportunity rate and the borrowing cost rate should be used where the surplus cash is foreseen to be available only for part of the period.

5. Tax relief may be available to offset the cost of borrowing and this should be reflected in the calculations. Where an organisation is not subject to tax, no adjustment will be required.

Tax delays

The period of the delay in receiving tax relief is one of the most important elements in the evaluation of any borrowing or lease decision. All companies now have to wait nine months from the end of their financial year in order to benefit, but it is possible to accelerate the benefits with judicious use of group relief provisions. (This was considered in detail in Chapter 5.)

In an evaluation, present values should be compared using different tax delay assumptions, as these will affect both the timing of cashflows themselves and the net of tax discount rate. Should the business temporarily be in a non-tax paying position, the period of the delay may be significantly longer. A before-tax discount rate may be required for the period during which the company ceases to be in a tax paying position. When using a before-tax discount rate, it will be necessary to adjust the derived present value for the notional tax on the interest carried forward to the first payment date.

Failure to predict the correct tax payment dates accurately will have a significant impact on the net of tax borrowing, as shown in the table following.

Gross rate before tax	Period of tax delay in months			
	0	17	27	39
10	6.5%	6.8%	7.0%	7.2%
12	7.7%	8.2%	8.5%	8.8%
14	9.1%	9.7%	10.1%	10.5%

The table illustrates the effect of delaying the benefit of tax relief, with corporation tax at, say, 35 per cent.

Other considerations

A short period lease of, say, three years' duration will have the effect of writing off the asset because, providing that the contract can be commercially justified, the rentals will qualify for tax relief. If the asset is to be retained for longer than the period defined in section 57 of the Finance Act 1985, de-pooling will not be possible with the result that it will be more than a decade before full tax relief can be obtained on the purchase cashflow.

For the company anticipating profits falling within the higher marginal rate band, advance rentals will be worth considering because these may be deductible from profits otherwise taxed at a higher rate.

However, before venturing into a structure which could be deemed by the Revenue to be uncommercial, due regard should be made to the true motive behind the selected period, in order to avoid the possibility that the rentals may have to be respread over the life of the asset in the tax computation.

Companies which anticipated paying little or no tax may find a long period lease, of say ten years, to be attractive, but a future settlement figure may prove to be costly if there is a chance that the asset may be disposed of during the basic lease term.

The Inland Revenue disclosed its future approach to the lessee's structured rentals in a Statement of Practice during April 1991. Professional guidance should be sought before a major change is undertaken in the way a business accounts for its lease rentals.

Comparison of the alternative products

It will be possible to compare outright purchase, with leasing products and the alternatives of hire purchase finance or bank loan. For the purposes of the illustrations that follow (Examples 9.2, 9.3 and 9.4) it is assumed that the hire purchase and the bank loan cashflow will be the same.

It should, however, be borne in mind that banks will frequently require a facility fee to be paid upon acceptance of the offer by the customer, and the finance company may vary the amount or the timing of the option to purchase fee in lease purchase. This has not been taken into account. Had it been, it would have improved the leasing benefit, because of the effect of the fees payable at the very beginning, or during some other point, of the cashflow.

The purchase illustrations have been run on for a period of ten years and the resultant cashflows have then been discounted back to a net present value at the end of the comparative basic lease period. Clearly this is only one method of evaluation, but the authors believe it to be representative of the approach taken in some major organisations.

No attempt has been made to predict the Revenue's approach to SSAP 21 accounting following the Statement of Practice issued on 11 April 1991, since it would appear that individual accounting policies will be followed and the variety of possibilities would make simple illustration unduly complex.

Example 9.2 A comparison of the benefits of leasing versus outright purchase: nine month tax delay

Company year-end	December
Company tax delay	nine months
Lease inception date	1 December 1991
Purchase cost	£1,000.00
Lease rental value	£48.00
Number of rentals	24
Rental frequency	Monthly
Rentals payable in	Advance
First rental	£144.00
Discount rate percentage	12%
Corporation tax	33%
Writing down allowance	25%

Accrual accounting methods have been used and tax computations are made to a minimum unit of one month.

Lease cashflow:
summary of the comparison

	Lease	Purchase
	£	£
Total outlay	1,248.00	1,000.00
Tax relief	411.84	287.57
Net outlay	836.16	712.43
Net present value (NPV)	805.92	773.51
Net benefit		32.42

Lease cashflow

No.	Period	Rental payment £	Tax relief on rentals £	Cash flow £	Cumulative cost £	Discounted cashflow £	Net present value £
1	Dec–91	144.00		144.00	144.00	144.00	144.00
2	Jan–92	48.00		48.00	192.00	47.52	191.52
3	Feb–92	48.00		48.00	240.00	47.05	238.58
4	Mar–92	48.00		48.00	288.00	46.59	285.17
5	Apr–92	48.00		48.00	336.00	46.13	331.29
6	May–92	48.00		48.00	384.00	45.67	376.96
7	Jun–92	48.00		48.00	432.00	45.22	422.18
8	Jul–92	48.00		48.00	480.00	44.77	466.95
9	Aug–92	48.00		48.00	528.00	44.33	511.28
10	Sep–92	48.00		48.00	576.00	43.89	555.17
11	Oct–92	48.00	47.52	0.48	576.48	0.43	555.60
12	Nov–92	48.00		48.00	624.48	43.02	598.63
13	Dec–92	48.00		48.00	672.48	42.60	641.22
14	Jan–93	48.00		48.00	720.48	42.18	683.40
15	Feb–93	48.00		48.00	768.48	41.76	725.16
16	Mar–93	48.00		48.00	816.48	41.34	766.50
17	Apr–93	48.00		48.00	864.48	40.94	807.44
18	May–93	48.00		48.00	912.48	40.53	847.97
19	Jun–93	48.00		48.00	960.48	40.13	888.10
20	Jul–93	48.00		48.00	1,008.48	39.73	927.83
21	Aug–93	48.00		48.00	1,056.48	39.34	967.17
22	Sep–93	48.00		48.00	1,104.48	38.95	1,006.12
23	Oct–93	48.00	190.08	(142.08)	962.40	(114.15)	891.97
24	Nov–93	48.00		48.00	1,010.40	38.18	930.15
25	Dec–93				1,010.40		930.15
26	Jan–94				1,010.40		930.15
27	Feb–94				1,010.40		930.15

No.	Period	Capital outlay £	Tax relief on capital allowances £	Cash flow £	Cumulative cost £	Discounted cashflow £	Net present value £
28	Mar–94				1,010.40		930.15
29	Apr–94				1,010.40		930.15
30	May–94				1,010.40		930.15
31	Jun–94				1,010.40		930.15
32	Jul–94				1,010.40		930.15
33	Aug–94				1,010.40		930.15
34	Sep–94				1,010.40		930.15
35	Oct–94		174.24	(174.24)	836.16	(124.23)	805.92

Purchase cashflow

No.	Period	Capital outlay £	Tax relief on capital allowances £	Cash flow £	Cumulative cost £	Discounted cashflow £	Net present value £
1	Dec–91	1,000.00		1,000.00	1,000.00	1,000.00	1,000.00
2	Jan–92				1,000.00		1,000.00
3	Feb–92				1,000.00		1,000.00
4	Mar–92				1,000.00		1,000.00
5	Apr–92				1,000.00		1,000.00
6	May–92				1,000.00		1,000.00
7	Jun–92				1,000.00		1,000.00
8	Jul–92				1,000.00		1,000.00
9	Aug–92				1,000.00		1,000.00
10	Sep–92				1,000.00		1,000.00
11	Oct–92		82.50	(82.80)	917.50	(74.69)	925.31
12	Nov–92				917.50		925.31
13	Dec–92				917.50		925.31
14	Jan–93				917.50		925.31
15	Feb–93				917.50		925.31
16	Mar–93				917.50		925.31
17	Apr–93				917.50		925.31
18	May–93				917.50		925.31
19	Jun–93				917.50		925.31
20	Jul–93				917.50		925.31
21	Aug–93				917.50		925.31
22	Sep–93				917.50		925.31
23	Oct–93		61.88	(61.88)	855.63	(49.71)	875.60
24	Nov–93				855.63		875.60
25	Dec–93				855.63		875.60
26	Jan–94				855.63		875.60
27	Feb–94				855.63		875.60
28	Mar–94				855.63		875.60
29	Apr–94				855.63		875.60
30	May–94				855.63		875.60
31	Jun–94				855.63		875.60
32	Jul–94				855.63		875.60
33	Aug–94				855.63		875.60
34	Sep–94				855.63		875.60
35	Oct–94		143.20	(143.20)	712.43	(102.10)	773.51

Example 9.3 A comparison of the benefits of leasing versus outright purchase: three month tax delay

Company year-end	December
Company tax delay	three months
Lease inception date	1 December 1991
Purchase cost	£1,000.00
Lease rental value	£48.00
Number of rentals	24
Rental frequency	Monthly
Rentals payable in	Advance
First rental	£144.00
Discount rate percentage	12%
Corporation tax	33%
Writing down allowance	25%

Accrual accounting methods have been used and tax computations are made to a minimum unit of one month.

Lease cashflow:
summary of the comparison

	Lease	Purchase
	£	£
Total outlay	1,248.00	1,000.00
Tax relief	411.84	287.57
Net outlay	836.16	712.43
Net present value (NPV)	786.24	759.57
Net benefit		26.67

Lease cashflow

No.	Period	Rental payment £	Tax relief on rentals £	Cash flow £	Cumulative cost £	Discounted cashflow £	Net present value £
1	Dec–91	144.00		144.00	144.00	144.00	144.00
2	Jan–92	48.00		48.00	192.00	47.52	191.52
3	Feb–92	48.00		48.00	240.00	47.05	238.58
4	Mar–92	48.00		48.00	288.00	46.59	285.17
5	Apr–92	48.00	47.52	0.48	288.48	0.46	285.63
6	May–92	48.00		48.00	336.48	45.67	331.30
7	Jun–92	48.00		48.00	384.48	45.22	376.52
8	Jul–92	48.00		48.00	432.48	44.77	421.29

No.	Period						
9	Aug–92	48.00		48.00	480.48	44.33	465.61
10	Sep–92	48.00		48.00	528.48	43.89	509.50
11	Oct–92	48.00		48.00	576.48	43.45	552.96
12	Nov–92	48.00		48.00	624.48	43.02	595.98
13	Dec–92	48.00		48.00	672.48	42.60	638.58
14	Jan–93	48.00		48.00	720.48	42.18	680.75
15	Feb–93	48.00		48.00	768.48	41.76	722.51
16	Mar–93	48.00		48.00	816.48	41.34	763.86
17	Apr–93	48.00	190.08	(142.08)	674.40	(121.17)	642.69
18	May–93	48.00		48.00	722.40	40.53	683.22
19	Jun–93	48.00		48.00	770.40	40.13	723.15
20	Jul–93	48.00		48.00	818.40	39.73	763.08
21	Aug–93	48.00		48.00	866.40	39.34	802.42
22	Sep–93	48.00		48.00	914.40	38.95	841.37
23	Oct–93	48.00		48.00	962.40	38.56	879.93
24	Nov–93	48.00		48.00	1,010.40	38.18	918.11
25	Dec–93				1,010.40		918.11
26	Jan–94				1,010.40		918.11
27	Feb–94				1,010.40		918.11
28	Mar–94				1,010.40		918.11
29	Apr–94		174.24	(174.24)	836.16	(131.87)	786.24

Purchase cashflow

No.	Period	Capital outlay £	Tax relief on capital allowances £	Cash flow £	Cumulative cost £	Discounted cashflow £	Net present value £
1	Dec–91	1,000.00		1,000.00	1,000.00	1,000.00	1,000.00
2	Jan–92				1,000.00		1,000.00
3	Feb–92				1,000.00		1,000.00
4	Mar–92				1,000.00		1,000.00
5	Apr–92		82.50	(82.50)	917.50	(79.28)	920.72
6	May–92				917.50		920.72
7	Jun–92				917.50		920.72
8	Jul–92				917.50		920.72
9	Aug–92				917.50		920.72
10	Sep–92				917.50		920.72
11	Oct–92				917.50		920.72
12	Nov–92				917.50		920.72
13	Dec–92				917.50		920.72
14	Jan–93				917.50		920.72
15	Feb–93				917.50		920.72
16	Mar–93				917.50		920.72
17	Apr–93		61.88	(61.88)	855.63	(52.77)	867.95
18	May–93				855.63		867.95
19	Jun–93				855.63		867.95
20	Jul–93				855.63		867.95
21	Aug–93				855.63		867.95
22	Sep–93				855.63		867.95
23	Oct–93				855.63		867.95
24	Nov–93				855.63		867.95

25	Dec–93			855.63		867.95
26	Jan–94			855.63		867.95
27	Feb–94			855.63		867.95
28	Mar–94			855.63		867.95
29	Apr–94	143.20	(143.20)	712.43	(108.38)	759.57

Commentary

These examples (Examples 9.2 and 9.3) demonstrate that, on the basis of the evaluation, the benefit of purchase will reduce the shorter the tax delay. In the cases in point, it would be up to the lessor to reduce the rental cost in order to provide the leasing advantage. Other assumptions will often alter the result.

No account has been taken of the cost of funds in the case of the outright purchase. Even if the customer is to rely upon capital provided by the business some due cognisance should be paid to the cost of funds employed in the acquisition, and this is best achieved by using a discount rate which reflects the cost of capital to the business. In this way, an analysis of the borrowings may then be avoided.

A similar approach can be made to compare leasing with lease purchase (or bank loan) and a further worked example is given in Example 9.4.

Example 9.4 A comparison of the benefits of leasing versus lease purchase: nine month tax delay

Company year-end	December
Company tax delay	nine months
Lease inception date	1 December 1991
Purchase cost	£1,000.00
Lease rental value	£47.00
Lease purchase rental	£49.50
Number of rentals	24
Rental frequency	Monthly
Rentals payable in	Advance
First rental-leasing	£143.00
First rental-lease purchase	£149.50
Discount rate percentage	12%
Corporation tax	25%
Writing down allowance	25%

Accrual accounting methods have been used and tax computations are made to a minimum unit of one month.

Summary of the comparison

	Lease	Lease purchase
	£	£
Total outlay	1,244.00	1,288.00
Tax relief	306.00	289.86
Net outlay	918.00	998.14
Net present value (NPV)	866.63	933.48
Net benefit	66.85	

Lease cashflow

No.	Period	Rental payment £	Tax relief on rentals £	Cash flow £	Cumulative cost £	Discounted cashflow £	Net present value £
1	Dec–91	143.00		143.00	143.00	143.00	143.00
2	Jan–92	47.00		47.00	190.00	46.53	189.53
3	Feb–92	47.00		47.00	237.00	46.07	235.61
4	Mar–92	47.00		47.00	284.00	45.62	281.23
5	Apr–92	47.00		47.00	331.00	45.17	326.39
6	May–92	47.00		47.00	378.00	44.72	371.11
7	Jun–92	47.00		47.00	425.00	44.28	415.38
8	Jul–92	47.00		47.00	472.00	43.84	459.23
9	Aug–92	47.00		47.00	519.00	43.40	502.63
10	Sep–92	47.00		47.00	566.00	42.97	545.60
11	Oct–92	47.00	35.75	11.25	577.25	10.18	555.79
12	Nov–92	47.00		47.00	624.25	42.13	597.91
13	Dec–92	47.00		47.00	671.25	41.71	639.62
14	Jan–93	47.00		47.00	718.25	41.30	680.90
15	Feb–93	47.00		47.00	765.25	40.89	721.81
16	Mar–93	47.00		47.00	812.25	40.48	762.29
17	Apr–93	47.00		47.00	859.25	40.08	802.38
18	May–93	47.00		47.00	906.25	39.69	842.06
19	Jun–93	47.00		47.00	953.25	39.29	881.35
20	Jul–93	47.00		47.00	1,000.25	38.90	920.26
21	Aug–93	47.00		47.00	1,047.25	38.52	958.78
22	Sep–93	47.00		47.00	1,094.25	38.14	996.91
23	Oct–93	47.00	141.00	(94.00)	1,000.25	(75.52)	921.39
24	Nov–93	47.00		47.00	1,047.25	37.39	958.78
25	Dec–93				1,047.25		958.78
26	Jan–94				1,047.25		958.78
27	Feb–94				1,047.25		958.78
28	Mar–94				1,047.25		958.78
29	Apr–94				1,047.25		958.78
30	May–94				1,047.25		958.78
31	Jun–94				1,047.25		958.78
32	Jul–94				1,047.25		958.78
33	Aug–94				1,047.25		958.78
34	Sep–94				1,047.25		958.78
35	Oct–94		129.25	(129.25)	918.00	(92.15)	866.63

Purchase cashflow

No.	Period	Rental payment	Tax relief on capital allowances + interest	Cash flow	Cumulative cost	Discounted cashflow	Net present value
		£	£	£	£	£	£
1	Dec–91	149.50		149.50	149.50	149.50	149.50
2	Jan–92	49.50		49.50	199.00	49.01	198.51
3	Feb–92	49.50		49.50	248.50	48.52	247.03
4	Mar–92	49.50		49.50	298.00	48.04	295.08
5	Apr–92	49.50		49.50	347.50	47.57	342.65
6	May–92	49.50		49.50	397.00	47.10	389.74
7	Jun–92	49.50		49.50	446.50	46.63	436.38
8	Jul–92	49.50		49.50	496.00	46.17	482.55
9	Aug–92	49.50		49.50	545.50	45.71	528.26
10	Sep–92	49.50		49.50	595.00	45.26	573.52
11	Oct–92	49.50	68.26	(18.76)	576.24	(16.98)	556.53
12	Nov–92	49.50		49.50	625.74	44.37	600.90
13	Dec–92	49.50		49.50	675.24	43.93	644.83
14	Jan–93	49.50		49.50	724.74	43.49	688.33
15	Feb–93	49.50		49.50	774.24	43.06	731.39
16	Mar–93	49.50		49.50	823.74	42.64	774.03
17	Apr–93	49.50		49.50	873.24	42.21	816.24
18	May–93	49.50		49.50	922.74	41.80	858.04
19	Jun–93	49.50		49.50	972.24	41.38	899.42
20	Jul–93	49.50		49.50	1,021.74	40.97	940.39
21	Aug–93	49.50		49.50	1,071.24	40.57	980.96
22	Sep–93	49.50		49.50	1,120.74	40.17	1,021.13
23	Oct–93	49.50	97.28	(47.78)	1,072.97	(38.38)	982.74
24	Nov–93	49.50		49.50	1,122.47	39.37	1,022.12
25	Dec–93				1,122.47		1,022.12
26	Jan–94				1,122.47		1,022.12
27	Feb–94				1,122.47		1,022.12
28	Mar–94				1,122.47		1,022.12
29	Apr–94				1,122.47		1,022.12
30	May–94				1,122.47		1,022.12
31	Jun–94				1,122.47		1,022.12
32	Jul–94				1,122.47		1,022.12
33	Aug–94				1,122.47		1,022.12
34	Sep–94				1,122.47		1,022.12
35	Oct–94		124.32	(124.32)	998.14	(88.64)	933.48

In this example leasing has been contrasted with lease purchase, but similar cashflows could have been generated by a bank loan, provided that the interest compounding periods were the same. This is a particularly important point when contrasting linked rate bank facilities with a fixed interest rate lease. The shorter the periods between the date of addition of interest the more expensive the funding cost will be.

Checklist items

The arguments surrounding lease versus purchase versus other funding arrangements will often be clouded by other issues. A simple checklist covering some of the major items to consider is as follows:

- Is ownership an important consideration?
- Is the asset to be recorded 'on balance sheet'?
- How long will the asset be of use to the business?
- Will the asset have a significant residual value upon disposal?
- What arrangements exist with the Inland Revenue regarding lease rentals?
- Does SSAP 21 affect the accounting or tax affairs?
- What is the opportunity cost of funds?
- Will it be necessary to borrow to acquire the asset or is it safe to use existing capital?
- What future expansion plans exist in the business?
- Who is to judge the performance of the business?
- What discount rate properly reflects the cost of funds to the business?

Summary

It should be stressed that every circumstance will depend upon the facts available at the time the decision needs to be made. Any arithmetic module is no more than that and will need to be kept up to date with the events in the business as they occur.

The correct choice of discount rate and the accurate selection of the tax assumptions will be fundamental to the integrity of the conclusions reached from this type of evaluation.

CHAPTER 10

LEASE EVALUATION

Introduction

Accurate pricing of the product is fundamental to the success of the financier's business. On the one hand, the income generated by the transaction must be sufficient to cover the overheads, while (hopefully) generating a surplus – the profit to be retained in the business for future growth. On the other hand, if the price is too high good quality business may be forfeited to a competitor.

The key to successful pricing is to understand the customer's needs and to develop a relationship built upon the added value which that understanding generates. Cost will always be a primary consideration, but flexibility, convenience and the most advantageous structure for the specific transaction will rank high in importance in the customer's mind. Many lessees prefer to remain with the same lessor because of the quality of service they receive, resulting from the understanding of their business which the lessor has built up over a period of time.

Factors affecting pricing

The main factors in pricing a transaction are the cost of funds, marketing costs, administrative overheads, bad debt provisions and profit anticipation. Each of these areas is considered below.

1. *The cost of funds*: Generally it is the cost of funding the lease which will prove to be the largest expense. Depending upon the nature of the lessor's portfolio and the size and term of the lease, options range from taking out matching loans at fixed interest rates (with the possible advantage of building in a SWAPS option) to funding from a general pool at floating interest rates. In each case it will be necessary to estimate the cost of funds in the lease, and

from this standpoint, fixed rate funding can be seen as advantageous because of its predictability compared with a linked rate alternative.

2. *Direct marketing costs*: The cost of acquiring the business falls within this category. Costs may include an element of legal fees in the larger transactions, while in the small transaction, commissions to introductory sources may be payable.

3. *Administrative overheads*: Head office costs, branch costs, both fixed and variable, will be included in this category, and the rates offered will need to include a provision to recover that outlay.

4. *Bad debt provisions*: The size of the provision in respect of bad debt will be determined by previous experience of that part of the portfolio. It may be expected to be lower for big ticket transactions than for those in the everyday smaller end of the market. This is because of the care taken to assess detailed credit and accounting information for higher value deals.

5. *Profit margin*: The margin required will depend upon the return which can be achieved in other areas of activity and upon the level of competition in that part of the marketplace. The lessor may be prepared to accept a smaller margin on its leasing facilities provided to a specific large customer, if other more profitable business is conducted with the same customer and the leases represent only one part of a package of services.

Factors affecting the lease cashflow

The lease cashflow will include a number of regularly recurring cash inflows and cash outflows, all of which will need to be taken into account in arriving at the overall earning potential of the contract.

The initial investment is the cost of the equipment which is to be leased, and it will be treated as a negative cashflow as it represents money paid out by the lessor. There may also be a dealer commission (or an introductory commission) which will be a negative cashflow and which will be included in the lease evaluation at the time that it is payable.

Interest will be charged on the outstanding balance of the capital invested in the lease. The method of calculation adopted will vary, but the interest will be debited to the lease cashflow (compounded) at regular intervals.

The timing of the capital allowances will depend upon the lessor's own tax position, and the possibility of accelerating the timing of the benefit of the allowance by the use of group relief. These will be positive cashflows and will reduce the outstanding capital. Allowances will be calculated as a cash amount at the assumed corporation tax rate of the lessor, for example:

Cost of equipment = £1,000.00
WDA at 25% = £250.00
£250.00 × (corporation tax rate) 35% = £87.50

The periodic flow of rentals will be that necessary to satisfy the profit requirement of the lessor for the initial investment after all periodic cashflows have been taken into account.

The lessor will wish to take profit from the lease at specific points in the contract (known as profit takeout). When this is done the capital balance outstanding in the lease will be increased. The lessor has a number of alternatives in calculating the cash profit takeout which include the following:

1. The actuarial method after tax.
2. The actuarial method before tax.
3. The breakeven cost of funds method.

Each of these methods will be considered below.

The actuarial method after tax

Examples 10.1 and 10.2 illustrate the case of a lessor company with a year ending on 31 December which writes a five year lease for equipment which qualifies for a writing down allowance of 25 per cent. It is assumed that the lessor has to wait nine months from the end of the financial year before the allowances are received and that the rate of corporation tax is 35 per cent throughout. The lessor has access to funds at 10 percent.

Example 10.1 Lessor's profit takeout (after tax)

Date	Rentals	Asset cost	Interest cost	Tax	Profit takeout	Cumulative cashflow
	£	£	£	£	£	£
31 Dec. 89	240	−1,000				−760
31 Dec. 90	240		−76	88	−7	−515
31 Dec. 91	240		−52	9	−5	−323
31 Dec. 92	240		−33	−16	−3	−135
31 Dec. 93	240		−14	−35	−1	55
31 Dec. 94			4	−51		8
31 Dec. 95				− 2		

Example 10.2 Lessor's tax computation

Year	1989	1990	1991	1992	1993	1994	1995	Total
Rental income (£)		240	240	240	240	240		1200
Tax depreciation (£)	(250)	(188)	(141)	(105)	(79)	(237)		(1,000)
Interest costs (£)		(76)	(52)	(33)	(14)	4		(171)
Taxable income (£)	(250)	(24)	47	102	147	7		29
Corporation tax (£)	88	9	(16)	(35)	(51)	(2)		(7)

The actuarial profit takeout rate is 0.95 per cent after tax, and this is the after tax earning on the funds employed by the lessor in this lease. The main assumption is that the lessor has adequate taxable profits to be able to claim tax relief in the first year. Clearly without this relief, there would be no profit from the transaction for the lessor.

The assumption has been made that the lessor can reinvest surplus funds at the 10 per cent interest cost. In practice a lessor may take a more conservative view and employ a lower interest rate.

The actuarial method before tax

An alternative method favoured by some lessors is to take out the margin as if it were taxed income (the actuarial profit takeout before tax method). Tax is then paid on the margin. The chief advantage of this method is that it saves the need to gross up after tax margins to compare them with equivalent before tax margins earned on loan business.

The breakeven cost of funds method

There is also the breakeven cost of funds method (also referred to as the dual rate of return method). Here, the interest rate assumed for cost of funds is varied until the lease just reaches a breakeven position. It gives the maximum interest rate that the lease can stand without generating a loss. The method computes the rate implicit in the lease rather than the margin to be achieved.

Each of the profit takeout methods provide similar information to the breakeven cost of funds when the after tax rate is grossed up at the tax rate used.

Margin, profit and funds employed

Broadly, the longer the lease period, the more profit that can be generated from the lease. This is because the funds are employed for longer periods and because market forces permit a higher margin to be applied for longer period contracts, reflecting potentially greater risk to the lessor.

The lessor will want to balance the portfolio, bearing in mind the lessor's particular tax position, the availability of matched funds for the respective periods and the ultimate credit risk.

At its simplest, if a lessor has ample taxable capacity, matched funding available and no significant credit risk, longer leases are attractive as they are likely to employ larger amounts of capital, reflecting the more substantial items of plant appropriate to the longer term contract, and which will realise a higher margin. On the other hand, the lessor will need to write business over a range of periods in order not to depend excessively upon a single category of business when market forces change.

The lessor will need to avoid replacing all of the loans employed in the business at the same time. If this is not done, sooner or later the cost of borrowing will move against the lessor with the risk that the opportunity for profit from the leasing portfolio is wiped out.

Structuring

A lease will often be structured to offer the greatest cashflow advantage to the lessee while maximising the lessor's tax situation. For example, a farmer may find it attractive to pay seasonally adjusted rentals which are higher at points in the year when the results of various harvests become available. The same may be true of tour operators and aircraft charter companies which may elect to pay larger rentals in the summer months.

This is generally accepted by the Revenue, provided that there is commercial justification and the business has adopted this approach historically. The structure will be varied with the particular circumstances of the lessee or the lessor.

If the lessee is to compare the lease quotation by reference to the rate implicit in the lease (the internal rate of return of the lease), longer periods, possibly with a balloon rental at the end, will improve the chance of winning the business because of the impact of the time which elapses before the rentals are due. However, should a lessee be planning some major capital outlay on a new manufacturing line, rentals which escalate in the early years may prove to be attractive as they can then be met out of future cashflows when production has reached maximum capacity. The extent of the escalation will be subject to review by the Revenue as to its reasonableness in the light of prevailing circumstances, because the tax arising on the rental stream will be deferred until later years.

An enhanced initial rental can be attractive to the lessee who has a corporation tax liability as it will be relieved against that liability, but any enhancement will need to be commercially based. If the Revenue consider the enhancement to have been affected for the purposes of tax deferment, it is likely to be respread over the anticipated life of the asset, or, at worst, disallowed completely.

To further enhance profitability while maintaining a competitive market position, a lessor which is part of a group will almost certainly wish to set up a number of leasing companies with different tax year-ends, in order that the claim for allowances can be made as quickly as possible. This organisation structure should provide the opportunity to pass back at least a proportion of the tax losses, arising as a result of capital allowances, to set off against the profits of other profitable group companies with earlier year-ends.

The lessor's exposure to changes in tax rates

The volume of taxable income increases throughout the basic lease term. Therefore, if there is an alteration in the rate of corporation tax, the lessor will need to reflect this change in the rental profile in order to preserve the post-tax margin. There are several methods which will recoup the tax variation cost (or calculate a subsequent rental refund where the movement in tax rate favours the lessor). The method chosen will depend upon the lease documentation itself.

Method 1 involves the calculation of the tax variation during the financial accounting period, including tax on the variation, using the gross cashflow as a base. In Method 2 the cashflow of the lease is rerun to recalculate the outstanding rentals, thereby preserving the net margin. The benefit of this is that, whatever happens to the rates of tax, the lessor will have preserved a net return. Preserving only the gross margin means there would still be a liability to tax variations. With Method 3 a lessee may be required to make a single one-off payment to reflect the effect of the variation in the rate of tax during the financial accounting period. The reference point for the calculation of the sum payable could relate to either the net return or the gross margin.

Documentation of tax variation

The larger the value of the transaction, the more complex the documentation in respect of tax variations will be. Indeed it is still common practice for the lessor to exclude tax variation from low value contracts because of the disproportionately high cost of collecting the variation when the outstanding capital is modest.

Some contract hire companies prefer to use an indexation geared to an inflationary factor which is periodically applied to all rental profiles rather than to become involved in recalculating rental streams for individual contracts.

Leases linked to a cost of money

In times of high interest rates, may lessees will want to have the benefit of paying reduced rentals when money rates fall. Traditionally, finance house base rate was used as a measure of cost of money, but as the market has grown increasingly competitive, many lessors have sought a more up-to-the minute measure of the cost of funds. Depending upon the lessor selected, rentals will be quoted using one of the London Interbank Offered Rates (LIBORs) or a bank base rate.

Rentals will be priced using an assumed, or notional cost of funds, and will remain fixed while the actual cost of funds, as published, remains equal to the notional money cost. Adjustments will then be made when cost of money ceases to be equal to the notional rate. There are very many permutations on the market, and the prospective lessee will need to exercise caution in assessing such opportunities. Questions to ask the salesperson include the following:

- When will the adjustment be payable?
- How is the interest to be charged and over what period will it be compounded?
- How will the rental refund be computed and when is it payable?
- What is the effect of tax variation on these adjustments?
- How is the figure for LIBOR arrived at? Is it calculated on the day of lease inception, or at some other point?
- How is an early settlement quotation calculated?
- Can rentals remain fixed through a band of interest rates in order to minimise the number and frequency of adjustments made?
- Is there an opportunity to lock into a fixed rental stream later on when rates fall (a drop lock facility) and, if so, what is the cost?

- Is there a minimum rate below which refunds will not be made and is there a maximum rate above which additional charges will not be made?
- Can the lease be extended when rates go up, rather than the lessee having to pay additional or enhanced rentals?

Advance quotations on fixed terms

Increasingly the lessee, who is about to undertake a large project taking several months to complete, will need to be able to forecast accurately the cost of rentals in a given set of circumstances. This has led to the common practice of quoting on the basis of floating to drawdown.

Here, subject to some modification by individual lessors, the practice is to quote a fixed rental on the assumption of a specific cost of money and an express date on which the lease is to commence. Once the lease has been incepted the rentals will then remain fixed for money cost, but the lease rate will only crystallise at the point of the completion of the documentation, being determined by the actual cost of money at that time of completion. The initial quotation will include a factor which the lessee can use to adjust the rental upward or downward, in order to predict the rental cost against a specific cost of money at the time of inception (or drawdown) of the lease.

In large value transactions, it is usual to see quotations which define all possible movements in rental price, including those of tax variation. This is less common in the middle ticket sector, and almost unheard of at the smaller end of the market.

The profit areas of a lease

A financial lessor will derive profit from the lease itself. This is different from the supplier who offers leasing as a sales aid, because in these circumstances there will also be an opportunity for profit relating to the sale of goods at retail mark-up.

Within a finance lease, the lessor will have four areas of potential profit, as follows:

1. The basic lease period: wherein the lessor will expect to recoup the capital outlay together with finance charges, while benefiting from the capital allowances.
2. The renewal period (which is often at the lessee's option): rentals in this period will represent virtually pure profit in all but the most highly structured transactions.

3. The sharing of the sale proceeds: the lessor is required to retain a proportion of the sale proceeds in order to distinguish the lease from that of hiring with a purchase option in favour of the customer. The higher the proportion the lessor can negotiate, the greater will be the level of profit retained.

4. Fee income: the final area for profit results from the negotiation of fee income, in the form of facility or cancellation fees. Fees may be justified when the nature of the transaction requires a large amount of preparatory time, or a particularly large sum of money to be reserved to accommodate the transaction.

Additional income opportunities

In an attempt to offer a complete service, while maximising income producing opportunities, lessors may sometimes be willing to arrange supplementary insurance packages on preferential terms. Keyman-type policies have been on offer for a number of years, and there is an increase in other areas of insurance cover as a result of more active marketing by the parent banks of many lessors.

CHAPTER 11

✝

KEYMAN INSURANCE

Introduction

Many financiers will be able to grasp the opportunity to provide insurance related products to their customers at the point when they are concluding a financial transaction. Where the customer is less well established, perhaps a sole trader, or a sole trader who is about to form a limited liability company for the first time, the financier will generally introduce the life and personal accident insurance concept.

When the financier is a clearing bank, specific reference will often be made to the bank's own insurance arm from which an entire range of products can be obtained. This will usually include cover in respect of loss of profit, all risk liability, vehicle, building and contents, and pension funds, as well as Keyman policies.

Keyman policies

The asset financier will focus attention upon the Keyman policy, relating the pricing either to the asset cost or to the outstanding financial commitment, in one form or another. These policies are relatively inexpensive, but the terms upon which a claim will be accepted should be studied carefully, since some accident policies will only cover instalments for a part of the term of the finance agreement.

Types of insurance cover

The UK corporate market is still developing. There are two distinct types of cover available. These are Keyman cover and Keyman plus cover, which will be presented in a variety of forms depending upon the insurer with whom the financier has developed the product.

Where the business has a number of owner-directors, each may acquire a policy, subject to the rules laid down by the insurer relating to state of health and age. Alternatively, the operator of the equipment may prove difficult to replace in view of the nature of the skills required and a policy will be available to cover this individual.

Keyman cover

Keyman cover is the simplest type of product. It will be designed to pay off the total outstanding liability under the financial contract at the time of the death of the insured person, subject to certain exclusions.

In common with most general life policies which do not require a medical, existing conditions and specific conditions, such as AIDS, will be excluded. There will be a ceiling above which a medical examination will be required. This may be as high as £100,000 but will vary from company to company.

Premiums will usually be at a fixed rate per £1,000 financed, but may be rounded to the nearest £1,000, providing the insured has not reached the age of 65 years before the maturity of the contract. Cover will generally apply to the instalments payable, rather than the original cost of the asset. In other words, its value will diminish as rentals or instalments are paid. This is rarely term insurance. A claim will only be accepted upon the death of the insured as evidenced by the death certificate.

Keyman plus cover

This type of policy will also pay out on the death of the insured, but will also cover other eventualities such as accident and sickness. It is therefore particularly beneficial to the owner-operator of an asset, the sole trader, or, on behalf of the company, the machine operator, since instalments will be met by the insurer. In this way the financial costs of an asset can be covered while it lays idle.

Policies should be checked carefully, since many insurers will limit the period over which they will agree to pay instalments or rentals. However, most, if not all, insurers will cover a period of at least twelve months for any one condition causing the incapacity, which in virtually every case will allow time in which to overcome the problem.

Current costs

It is never correct to generalise, but it would appear that Keyman policies, covering life only, will be charged at around 75p per month per £1,000 of cover. Keyman plus will cost £2 – £3 per month per £1,000 of cover, but reductions will often be available for the large transaction, following a medical examination of the proposed individual. The financier receives commissions of up to 30 per cent of the premium paid.

Tax considerations

Provided it can be proved that the premium is a legitimate business expense, and any settlement is to be made to the business rather than to the insured or his family, the business will probably be able to claim full tax relief on the premium. There will be potential problems in respect of a sole trader, and care should be taken to avoid a 'benefit in kind' assessment by the Revenue, in respect of either partners in a partnership, or owner-directors, in a family business.

Administration

Administration is very straightforward. Many documents will include a separate section for the insurance details. Those that do not will be accompanied by a short, simple proposal, usually accompanied by a separate direct debit mandate. In the latter case, payments will be debited directly by the insurance company, rather than in the former wherein the financier will act as agent for the insurer for the purposes of collection. In all cases, the financier will handle the initial enquiry in respect of a claim which will be pursued by the insurance company.

Reduction of the financier's risk

While it can be argued that a Keyman-type policy will add value to the financial package, it will add some level of comfort to the financier accepting the transaction, in so far as certain possible consequences of entering into the transaction may be avoided. It will not however be acceptable as a substitute for more tangible security.

The financier will often see the sale of insurance as an additional profit centre, since commission will be received from the insurance company. This may prove to be a lever for the customer in negotiating a reduction in the rate proposed for the finance.

Sales technique

The corporate insurance market is new to many financiers, although some suppliers offering finance will have experience which has been built up over a number of years.

The customer who is introduced to the insurance product will find that the salesperson usually adopts one of two routes: the assumptive sell and the disclosed route.

The sales techniques applied will vary from financier to financier, with those having their roots in the retail marketplace adopting what is known as the assumptive sell. In this scenario, the financier will quote a price inclusive of the insurance premium. Should the customer object on grounds of cost, then the fact that insurance protection is included will be disclosed. This will generally be coupled with a list of benefits to the customer designed to make a refusal difficult. While this may indeed be beneficial to the smaller business with only limited existing cover, cheaper quotations are generally available separately through insurance brokers, for those with the time and the expertise to select them.

With the disclosed route, the financier will include details of the cover available with the documentation provided at the point of incepting the finance contract. The customer is provided with a list of benefits and invited to apply for insurance at a modest premium.

As a condition in some cases, such as a management buyout, the financier may require Keyman insurance to be effected on the owners of the business as a condition of the financier's agreement to make funds available. This is distinct from using a sales pitch to encourage the customer to take up the policy.

Since the financier will earn a commission from the insurer, as well as having the comfort of knowing the debt will, at least in part, be repaid upon the occurrence of certain events, the financier will feel more inclined to grant the full facility required to an emerging business which depends upon the expertise of a small group of people.

Customer benefits

Keyman insurance will generally be available from the asset financier in respect of the directors of the business, or for the key personnel, for instance skilled operators of the assets financed.

The main benefits are listed below:

Directors	*Key personnel*

Keyman

Removes a part of the financial stress in the event of death of the principal.

The outstanding balance will be paid in the event of death.

Other shareholders in a family business are protected.

The period of disuse is covered, allowing time to find and train an operator.

Cashflow can be preserved at a time when sales may fall.

The business can review its operating procedures without financial pressures.

Keyman plus

The owner-operator can recover from accident or sickness without financial hardship.

Money is available to provide for a temporary manager.

Financial stress is removed during the absence of the operator.

Cash is released to assist with temporary staff wages.

All policies

Tax relief is available in most cases.

It is easy to arrange.

The claims procedure is simple.

Tax relief is available in most cases.

It is easy to arrange.

The claims procedure is simple.

Summary

Keyman insurance is particularly popular with the owner-driver whose income depends upon the ability to work. The policies should never be substituted for adequate insurance against all the risks involved in becoming a self-employed sole trader. They do however represent a useful buffer against unexpected accident or sickness over a short period, providing the peace of mind that goes with knowing that the instalments will be met on time.

For the larger proposal, it would seem that benefit may be derived from an approach to an insurance broker for a bespoke quotation for term life cover. This should show a significant saving over the standard policy terms offered by the financier, provided the insured is relatively young and has a good health record.

CHAPTER 12

SALES-AID SCHEMES

Introduction

As discussed earlier in the chapters on taxation, some manufacturers and suppliers offer finance terms for the acquisition of their equipment on their own account. In capital equipment markets, those that do not will often negotiate a sales-aid facility with a financier, to whom applications for extended terms will be passed for approval.

The market

In theory almost any type of capital equipment can be financed under a sales-aid scheme. In practice, assets as diverse as sign making machines, computers, earth moving equipment and telephone systems will be available on a supplier-finance package. The range of equipment is enormous and many financiers will give consideration to any application put forward by a reputable and established supplier.

Market specialisation

Over recent years some lessors have established themselves as specialist sales-aid businesses. In so doing, they have learned the skills required to credit approve transactions swiftly and without taking undue risk. This is a key area in the relationship between the supplier and the financier. The supplier will hope that every transaction will be approved since each will represent a sale at retail price on cash terms.

The financier will need to maintain good records of the status of the accounts with customers from any one source. If the quality of the business introduced by a particular supplier starts to fall, then the financier will be faced with potential bad debts and resultant losses from the contracts placed by the supplier. There are potential pitfalls relating to the customers' rights under consumer legislation should the supplier fail to replace or repair faulty goods.

It is for these reasons that the financier will resist entering into a relationship with a newly formed supplier whose track record has yet to be established. The specialist sales-aid company will have become adept at seeking out the quality supplier and will have established systems which act swiftly to approve and to collect its debts.

The options

Although there are a great many bespoke applications in the market, each tailored to the product, its anticipated life and the supplier's market niche, all will ultimately boil down to either a lease or a hire purchase contract. Operating leasing transactions are developing rapidly where the asset has a predictable depreciation pattern based upon use. A few examples of sales-aid finance packages are given below.

Operating contracts: motor vehicles

Probably the most common, and therefore the best known, option is that of motor vehicle contract hire. Many vehicle dealers will now offer their own contracts, but those that chose not to will be able to arrange facilities through a major finance house. In the latter case, the operating nature of a lease will often be constructed by the supplier (dealer) agreeing to repurchase the vehicle at the end of the term at an agreed residual percentage. The percentage will be large enough to satisfy the tests applied by SSAP 21. The dealer will then dispose of the returned vehicle in the second user market generating a further profit opportunity.

There are a number of options available in the contract hire market and these include the following:

- Supply of the vehicle only,
- Supply of the vehicle with maintenance,
- Supply of the vehicle with maintenance and a replacement vehicle option,
- As above, plus membership of a motoring organisation and provision of vehicle excise duty.

Operating contracts: plant

Most contractors will hire the plant they need for a specific contract over the period of the contract. If they need high value road building machines for a two year period, but the life expectancy of the equipment exceeds, say, five years, they are more likely to hire than to purchase for all the accepted budgetary and financial reasons.

An operating contract will be ideal in many such situations. The customer will pay for use rather than ownership, and the supplier will often arrange a lease for the period of the underlying contract, and then repurchase in the same way as for a motor dealer at the end of the term.

Operating contracts: computers

This is a very specialist area, since many small systems will depreciate rapidly, or become obsolescent during the term of the hiring. Large mainframe systems do have a value to the specialist financier, and contracts allowing for an upgrade of the central processing unit (CPU) during the contract period are not unusual. When the customer exercises the option to upgrade, the old CPU will then be configured in another system on hire elsewhere.

Because of the high level of technical expertise required, this is almost exclusively the province of specialists – either manufacturer or finance based.

Finance leases and hire purchase

An enormous range of equipment is available on finance terms. At its simplest the salesperson will produce the financier's document at the point of sale and, upon completion, this will be forwarded to the financier for credit approval. The financier will then search the credit registers for evidence of a track record and may take up bank references. If the requirement is substantial audited accounts will be required.

Upon approval (which usually takes no more than two working days for modest transactions), the supplier will invoice the financier and arrange for delivery and installation. The benefit to the supplier, apart from overcoming the customer's price objections, is that payment will be received as soon as the customer has signed a satisfaction note in respect of the equipment. The alternative might have been to reduce the price, or to provide extended payment terms in order to achieve the sale.

Some suppliers may receive a commission from the financier, either based upon the value of individual transactions, or the total volume of individual transactions within an agreed period (a volume bonus), or both. Its extent depends upon the financier's margin and the overall value placed upon the quality of the business received from the supplier source. Where commission is payable, it may be subject to a form of debit back should the customer fail in meeting the contractual obligations.

Alternative methods

Agency for undisclosed principle

The sales-aid dealer, who is in a position to introduce several million pounds worth of introductions, may negotiate a facility with the financier to act as the agent of the financier for the collection of rentals. The documentation will be drawn up in the house style of the dealer, but the terms and conditions will be those of the financier.

The financier will act as principle for the transaction, providing both the funding and, in the case of a lease, the tax shelter, but will not be disclosed to the customer unless there is a serious breach of the terms of the contract. The dealer will invoice the financier and receive payment as described above, but the dealer will also be responsible for collecting the customer payments and passing over all sums due to the financier on the due dates.

This method is of particular benefit to the dealer who provides full maintenance on the equipment, since the customer will pay only one rental and will have only one document, and the dealer will be able to retain all payments other than that proportion due to the financier.

From the financier's point of view, the administration of the account will remain the principal responsibility of the dealer, thereby reducing the financier's administration. There may be some limited recourse to the dealer in the event of customer default, and an agreement that the dealer must use all best endeavours to dispose of the equipment and account to the financier for the proceeds upon determination of the contract.

Overprinted documentation

Provided the business volume is expected to justify the cost, the dealer's logo may be over-printed onto the financier's documentation. However, there is a risk to the financier, since this will further bind the financier to the dealer in the event of a dispute, and it will be necessary for the financier to be satisfied that the objectives and business style of the dealer and the financier are compatible.

Controlling legislation

The Consumer Credit Act 1974 will govern transactions with unincorporated bodies (mainly partnerships and sole traders) where the transaction is below a certain size. Currently the limits are as follows:

1. Leasing: the rentals payable under the contract (including VAT at the rate in force when the contract is established) must not exceed £15,000.
2. Hire purchase: the balance financed must not exceed £15,000.

Where a transaction falls within the Act, the dealer and the financier will each be liable for the quality of the merchandise and for its fitness for the purpose for which it was supplied. This is particularly important where the dealer goes out of business, for the financier will become liable for the maintenance of the equipment and for its repair if circumstances apply.

There will be a period during which the customer has a right to withdraw from the agreement upon its signing if the contract was completed away from trade premises. If goods are supplied and paid for within this period and the customer gives notice of cancellation, they must be collected by the financier and any sums paid or goods given in consideration of a deposit must be returned to the customer. The financier will therefore need to exercise care to see that the dealer has complied with the requirements of the Act and that all documentation has been completed accurately in the prescribed format.

There are stringent regulations regarding the advertising of facilities in the consumer market, and the financier will need to set up a system to review all advertising material used by the dealer, since the dealer will be equally liable for any breach of the regulations in a sales-aid relationship.

Benefits and disadvantages

Benefits to the dealer of sales-aid schemes include the following:

- The dealer will be able to negotiate finance terms which help to overcome the customer's price objections.
- The dealer will be seen to offer a simple and convenient package which can be tailored to suit the customer's needs.
- The dealer will be able to minimise the discounts given and will be paid immediately the transaction is complete.

- The dealer's reputation will be enhanced by arranging the finance package with a major financier.
- There may be a commission-based profit opportunity.
- The financier will provide a full training package for the dealer's staff.

Benefits to the financier of sales-aid schemes include the following:

- There will be an opportunity to increase the customer database and to sell additional facilities.
- By negotiating facilities through a variety of dealers, the financier will spread the risk among a range of industries and a range of product lines.
- The potential cost of obtaining a new customer will be reduced.

Disadvantages to the dealer of sales-aid schemes include the following:

- Some control is lost while the financier considers the credit risk.
- The dealer's staff will need additional skills to close a finance deal.
- A deal may be lost because the customer does not approve of the financier.

Disadvantages to the financier of sales-aid schemes include the following:

- The dealer may breach legislation and involve the financier in legal costs or adverse publicity.
- A failure by the dealer may reflect badly on the financier.
- Introductions may be fraudulently manipulated to seek approval.

Protection for the parties of a sales-aid scheme

The financier will want to be satisfied that the product is reliable and that the dealer is capable of providing a high level of aftersales support. National coverage will be preferred to cater for the customer who relocates to a new area. The dealer should be well established with a clearly defined management structure and an ethical salesforce. The financier will need to be satisfied of the financial stability of the dealer's business.

The dealer will want a prompt and efficient customer service which extends to settlement quotations, technical assistance and a professional training package. The dealer will need to be assured that the financier understands the product range and the marketplace. Above all, consistency in pricing and credit control will be required in order that the dealer's own salesforce will remain committed to, and motivated by, the relationship.

The sales-aid contract

It is advisable for both parties to put the basis of their relationship into a formal contract. This will define the responsibilities of each party and periods of notice which either should give to the other in specific circumstances.

A quality, experienced financier and a professional dealer can substantially increase their business volumes as a result of the symbiosis between them.

Sharing responsibility for default

The financier will run an established trade and will therefore be equipped to deal with matters arising on customer default. However, the dealer's relationship with the customer will be placed in jeopardy if the default is merely of a technical nature. As a result the dealer should be prepared to take responsibility for the initial contact in such circumstances, even if this is not demanded by the financier.

Where the contract is in the form of an undisclosed agency, the dealer will be responsible for initial action. Failure to assist the financier will risk the dealer's maintenance payments where the financier collects maintenance, since the financier is likely to 'freeze' amounts due to the dealer for as long as the account is in default.

Types of default

Default can take a number of forms, some of which are detailed as follows:

1. A technical error arising in circumstances such as the customer changing bank accounts. The dealer should be able to resolve this problem without the intervention of the financier.
2. An error in payment of an invoice or standing order. The dealer should be able to resolve this problem without the intervention of the financier.
3. A payment stopped by the customer. This may be the result of a dispute between the dealer and the customer, in which event the situation is likely to be resolved more effectively by the dealer.
4. A cheque returned through lack of funds. This is an early warning sign of potential problems and action as soon as the default comes to light will improve the chances of collection.
5. A direct debit or standing order unpaid through lack of funds. This is an

early warning sign of potential problems and action as soon as the default comes to light will improve the chances of collection.
6. A direct debit not applied for. This will be due to the financier's error, and the customer will be more likely to appreciate action and assistance from the dealer than a call from the financier's accounts department, as previous negotiations will have been conducted with the dealer.

If there is a guarantor to the transaction, contact should be established at the same time as with the customer, and on no account should the terms be amended with the customer without the guarantor's agreement. The guarantee is likely to become worthless if the guarantor is not agreeable to any amendment to the payment profile.

Summary

There will be many benefits to the dealer and to the financier, but each will need to be willing to build a close working relationship if the profit opportunities available are to be realised.

The financier should be willing to accompany the dealer on a customer visit when, because of the size of the transaction, specialist negotiating skills are needed to close the deal. However, there should be a close understanding of each others' business and the respective negotiating styles.

Local connections will prove to be important for larger transactions and this is likely to be the focus of the sales-aid specialist financier of the future.

CHAPTER 13

ARRANGING A FINANCIAL PACKAGE

Introduction

The purpose of this chapter is to explain where finance can be obtained, how contact is made with suitable financiers and how to prepare an acceptable case.

It is just as important for the customer to feel comfortable with the financier as it is for the financier to feel secure with the risk. If both have a good working relationship, then future requirements will be more easily catered for.

Preparation

The level of preparation necessary during the journey to arranging a financial package will be largely dependent upon the nature of the assets needed and the length of time the customer has been established.

There is no substitute for advice from a professional accountant when it comes to preparing detailed cashflows for a new project. The clearing banks will be able to provide assistance both by personal representation at the branch level and by way of printed brochures to the newly emerging business.

While it is not the objective of this book to produce an all-encompassing work for the individual establishing a new business for the first time, at least some of the experiences described in this chapter may prove to be of assistance.

The objective of the finance

The first part of the exercise will be to define why the finance is required. This will probably seem to be an obvious statement, but when tax considerations are taken into account, it may prove to be less so. While the applicant will know exactly what is proposed and why, a third party reading a document in a busy credit vetting department may not find the application so clear. In this respect, a credit application is analogous to entering a public examination in so far as there is no substitute for good planning in the written work, and no question should be left unanswered providing the examiner with a reason to 'fail' the application.

The underwriter will need to see that there is at least a reasonable probability that the debt will be repaid in line with the proposed term. Therefore cashflows should be accompanied with as much detail as is reasonably practical. Where management accounts are provided, it will avoid delays for questions if the basis upon which they have been computed are described in detail. It will be helpful to highlight any variances from the accounting policies used in the audited results.

As with any examination, pertinent notes should be kept. However, too much information can be as damaging as too little. If the asset is one which offers good security, of if the customer is approaching a lender who already has ample security, notes should be restricted.

The financial requirement

In the modern world of finance not every transaction will need to be supported by detailed financial analysis. For many years it has been possible to acquire vehicle finance through the dealer in the showroom, and many more asset types will be available through dealer finance in the future. The problem with this relatively easy credit is that the customer will rarely find unbiased advice and an understanding of the business needs of the moment. After all, the dealer's salesperson is there principally to sell more of the dealer's product, not to give financial advice.

While there will often be little to choose between the competing forms of finance in the medium term, when tax considerations are taken into account, the short-term effect on the cashflows of choosing the wrong finance plan can be significant. It will be important for the business applicant to recognise the real expertise of the salesperson, and to seek independent advice where necessary.

Equally, more small businesses (and some larger ones) fail because they use a bank overdraft in the good economic years only to find themselves with no alternative longer-term finance when things start to become difficult. Bank managers are increasingly under pressure to increase their lendings and will not always resist customer pressure for the apparently cheaper alternative while things are going well.

Independent Advice

None of the above is intended to be a comment upon the ability of any finance source to satisfy the need, but is merely stated to highlight the need for the customer to seek guidance from someone independent of the financier where circumstances dictate. The immediate contact will generally be made by the auditor of the business whose detailed understanding of its objectives will be paramount. The practitioner from the larger firm will work with other professionals in the case of major projects or newly established concerns.

Tax and cashflow considerations

The new business generally will be concerned with effective cash utilisation, since its profits will not have been determined yet. Outright purchase will mainly be unattractive since the business will want to conserve its members' investment to cater for work in progress and debtors (as well as stock in trade if the business is a manufacturer or a supplier of goods). Start up costs may have been substantial and the main concern will be to build a customer base.

The established business will have more detailed tax considerations based upon its previous trading record. Its product choice will be focused more upon its current tax situation and the available structures which may be relevant.

The asset type

To varying degrees lenders will pay attention to the asset type for which the funding is required. For example, they will recognise that small computers depreciate very rapidly and offer little security by way of disposal proceeds, should a transaction fall into arrears. As a result, some additional security may be required and this will often take the form of a guarantee. Conversely, most fleet-type vehicles have a predictable depreciation pattern which is geared to their level of use. Should the customer fall behind with the repayments, such an asset will have a resale value which will generally cover the outstanding balance due to the financier. In this situation a guarantee is less likely to be required.

It will be worth shopping around for the best financial package, since lenders have different policies, and some may apply a formula to the amount of their advance versus the net worth of the customer's business in establishing whether a guarantee will be necessary. Rates too will vary, particularly where finance is arranged through the supplier, since manufacturers will offer special promotions on specific products from time to time.

The source of funding

Having decided upon the requirements and produced the accounting information to support the investment, the customer will have a wide choice of potential sources of finance, the main sources being detailed below.

Clearing banks

While the clearing bank will advertise a wide range of services, it will not necessarily be prudent to seek all of the financial requirements from one source. There will always be a risk that the clearing banker will consider that sufficient funds have already been invested in a particular business, and it may be better to keep some facility available to cater for future cashflow problems.

Where the clearing bank is approached, its management will assess the cashflows and audited results (where appropriate) and will generally make proposals for a range of facilities. These may include the following:

1. Overdraft: which is intended to be short term in nature, fluctuating with the need to finance seasonal stock levels, work in progress and debtors.
2. Loan: which will be provided to cater for specific expenditure of a capital nature with repayment structured in a manner that can be accommodated within the future cashflows of the business.
3. Leasing: where the tax and cashflow positions of the business make it desirable, the clearing bank will be able to introduce its leasing specialist, who will attempt to structure a facility over a similar period to that of a loan.
4. Other facilities: there will be a full range of opportunities which might include factoring in the short term, to commercial mortgage in the long term, depending on the customer's needs, financial standing and the magnitude of the expenditure.
5. Security: banks tend to take security wherever possible, and will argue that such action will help them to provide for the future needs of the business quickly and with minimum formality.

The need for security should not unduly concern the customer since the clearing bank is a professional organisation whose staff are thoroughly trained and capable of understanding the business needs of their customers.

However, there will be circumstances where the customer may be better advised to seek an alternative source of funding facilities. This will sometimes apply where the expenditure relates to a specific asset or an expenditure programme in respect of a range of assets. For example if a customer wishes to acquire a computer for the office, some light commercial vehicles and a replacement lathe, the finance company may be able to provide a more flexible package than the clearing bank.

Finance companies

Finance company salespeople will have specific training in their area of activity and will generally have a detailed knowledge of asset types. This will help them to structure a repayment profile which will be geared to the needs of the business while, at the same time, reflecting the useful life of the asset in the particular business environment.

Their asset finance products will include the following:

1. Leasing: which will be available for periods of up to seven years (ten to fifteen years for major projects) with a renewal option beyond the initial period. Leasing facilities will usually be available on a fairly wide range of assets, on an operating basis which will not necessarily require full balance sheet disclosure.
2. Hire purchase, credit sale and conditional sale: hire purchase is now frequently referred to as lease purchase. The facility will be tailored in much the same way as leasing, but the tax and balance sheet considerations will be quite different.
3. Other facilities: many finance companies offer debtor finance in the form of factoring or block discounting and these facilities may assist the working capital requirement of a new project.
4. Security: the finance company will often be content to hold the asset in question as the main, or sole, security. Where an additional security is required, this will usually take the form of either inter-company or personal guarantees. As a result, the cost of perfecting security by way of mortgages or debentures, which may be required by the clearing bank, will be removed.

It will be rare for the finance company to charge setting-up or facility fees on everyday expenditure requirements. However, sometimes clearing banks do require a fee to be paid upon the acceptance of terms by the customer.

Supplier finance

Many suppliers of capital equipment will either offer finance, or be able to arrange finance, at the point of sale. Most expenditure, on items such as a fork truck, a single motor car or a computer, will be catered for within no more than a day or so, sometimes even while the sale is being concluded. Larger acquisitions will need to be underwritten with the aid of accounts and may take a week or more to process.

This will often prove to be a cost effective way to arrange facilities because, not only can everything be tied up at one meeting, but the dealer may offer some special discount in the finance package. The products available will include leasing and hire purchase in almost all cases, and some suppliers may offer rental or full contract hire with maintenance.

Making contact

Most businesses will have a working relationship with a member of their bank's management team, who will be willing to discuss the customer's needs.

Finance houses are basically selling organisations and the established business will soon find itself on mailing and telephone sales lists. The largest financiers will be subsidiaries of banks, most of which will have provided their sales staff with a thorough training in their marketplace. The smaller and regionalised finance companies will tend to have recruited their sales staff from the larger organisations, but their capacity for business may be restricted because of their resources.

Suppliers will be quick to introduce finance if they suspect they will lose the sale on grounds of a price objection by the customer. Both suppliers and finance operators will arrange a convenient visit to their customer within a short period.

Finance is a very competitive market, and it will always be worth obtaining more than one quote. However, if the customer wishes to acquire a range of assets over a period of time, it will be important to ascertain that the financier will be able to handle business throughout the entire period, since some smaller financiers offer terms on a seasonal basis.

Specialist financiers and suppliers may prove to be the most helpful in structuring transactions because of their specialist knowledge of the field of operation and the nature of the assets.

The Finance Houses Association and The Equipment Leasing Association will be willing to supply a list of their member organisations, together with the respective organisation's code of practice to which member companies have agreed to adhere.

The information which will be required by the prospective lender will be along the lines of the checklist set out in Example 13.1.

Example 13.1 Checklist of information required by a prospective lender

About the business

- Business name and trading style.
- Address and registered office.
- Contact name, status and telephone number.
- Nature of the business.
- When the business was established, and date it was limited.
- Parent company details.
- Name and address of principals (unless a quoted company).
- Experience and qualifications of management.
- Banker's name and address.
- Length of time with the bank.
- Details of spread of customers and suppliers.
- Geographical location and industry type of customers.
- Whether audited accounts are available (usually for three preceding years).
- Whether management accounts or project cashflows are available.
- Other lines of credit available.

About the proposal

- What is to be acquired?
- When is delivery?
- Has an order been placed?
- New or used assets?
- Who are the suppliers?
- Who manufactures the equipment?
- Is the equipment standard or bespoke?
- What is the computer software cost?
- How will the assets be used (what mileages for vehicles)?

- Where will the equipment be located?
- What servicing arrangements will be made?
- Does the equipment require highly trained operators?
- Is it for a new project or for replacement?
- What proportion will installation or training costs be?
- Will progress payments be required?
- Will the customer want to act as agent of the financier?
- Will the goods be sublet?
- Who will insure the equipment?
- Will any part of it be used abroad?
- Are any grants available?

About the installation

- Will the equipment be installed permanently in a building?
- If so, who owns the building?
- Is the building freehold or leasehold?
- Are there mortgages or debentures?
- Is the asset to be incorporated within something else?
- Is special preparatory site work to be included?
- Is the supplier experienced in this work?
- Can all parts be readily identified?
- Will the supplier install the equipment?
- Are special licences required?
- Is planning permission needed?
- Is it a tried and tested system?
- How easily could it be dismantled and removed?

CHAPTER 14

AN INTRODUCTION TO SSAP 21

History

Due to the substantial growth of leasing, SSAP 21 was introduced as a means to standardise the way in which lease transactions were accounted for. It attempted to rationalise the variety of methods previously used, while bringing UK accounting methods into line with the methods used in other advanced countries.

Finance leases place the lessee in virtually the same commercial situation as if borrowed funds had been used to finance the acquisition. Legal title remains vested with the lessor, and it is the lessor who is entitled to the capital allowances. The rentals payable under the lease will normally be sufficient to cover the lessor's investment in the leased asset, but the rentals, will to some degree, reflect the benefit arising from capital allowances.

Finance leases have therefore become an attractive way of acquiring the use of equipment, and this is no more so than in the case of businesses which would otherwise be unable to benefit from the allowances if they were to purchase the asset.

In the absence of a mandatory accounting standard, the methods adopted to account for lease contracts have become diverse. Some companies have chosen simply to deduct the rentals in the profit and loss account, on the basis of the manner in which they have accrued over time. This has resulted in accounts which have failed to reflect fully the amount of capital expenditure on assets used in the business, and the commitments related to them.

The method required by SSAP 21 is for the leased assets to be capitalised, resulting in the lessee recording the right to use the asset as if it were a fixed asset, and reflecting the obligation to pay future rentals as a liability. Capitalisation of leased assets has been a requirement in the United States for a number of years, and a comprehensive standard on accounting for leases was issued in the form of Federal Accounting Standard FAS 13 in 1976.

SSAP 21 was published in August 1984, following the issue of the exposure draft ED 29 by the Accounting Standards Committee in 1981. Lessees were required to make certain disclosures in the notes in the accounts on or after 1 July 1984. These were to include the amount and the maturity of obligations relating to finance leases, and the amount of commitments relating to operating leases. It was necessary to understand the technique of capitalisation and the other requirements of SSAP 21 in order to comply with the required disclosures. The accounting entries had to be reflected in the balance sheet, and in the profit and loss account, only with effect from periods beginning on or before 1 July 1987.

Definitions

There needed to be a clear method of identification of those transactions which were to come within the scope of SSAP 21, and leases were to be categorised as either, finance leases or operating leases.

The standard defines a lease as a 'contract between a lessor and a lessee for the hire of a specific asset'.

It is a feature of such contracts that title to the asset remains with the lessor, but that the right to use the asset if afforded to the lessee in return for the payment of rentals. The definition is extended to contracts in which one party retains title to the asset but permits another party to use it in return for specified payments. Thus, hire purchase contracts fall within the definition.

There is no exemption for leases between related parties, such as companies which are members of the same group, although there is no need to recognise assets made available for use for no payment.

There is a specific exclusion in respect of lease contracts concerning the right to explore or exploit natural resources (e.g. minerals and timber), and licensing agreements relating to intellectual property (e.g. patents, manuscripts and copyrights).

Leases of land and buildings do come within the scope of the standard and should be accounted for using the same rules as for other asset types.

The classification of leases

SSAP 21 distinguishes between two types of lease contracts as follows:

1. Finance leases which confer substantially all the risks and rewards of ownership of an asset to the lessee.

2. Operating leases comprising all other leases.

The requirements for accounting for finance leases are very different from those in respect of operating leases, thus the definition is of paramount importance.

SSAP 21 applies to arrangements relating to the use of the asset, rather than to legal contracts, and does not prescribe detailed rules of identification. It is therefore necessary to consider all aspects of a lease in order to classify it correctly. The true commercial substance of the transaction must be fully considered, whatever its appearance may seem to be.

In making the classification of a lease and its related payments, any options or alternatives which the lessee may exercise should be studied carefully. Should the terms of the option be such that the lessee's choice can be confidently predicted, the lease should be construed on the assumption that the lessee will follow the predictable course.

If the lessee has the option to purchase for a nominal sum before the end of the asset's useful working life, or if there is the alternative of a secondary period at a significantly reduced rental, then the assumption should be made that the lessee will execute this option. Conversely, if the lessee can only terminate upon payment of a substantial penalty, it should be assumed that the lessee will avoid the execution of the right to termination.

Many leases will be simple to classify. Where the lessor has only a very limited interest in the asset despite holding legal title to it, the lease will be a finance lease. In effect the lessor's rights have been exchanged for a stream of rentals. If, conversely, the lessor retains a significant interest in the equipment, then the lease is likely to be an operating lease. An example may be a self-drive car hire operation, since business may suffer if vehicles frequently breakdown or fail to meet targeted residual values.

Risks and rewards of ownership

Under a finance lease, the lessee enjoys substantially all the 'risks and rewards of ownership'. These include those arising during the period in which the lessee has the use of the asset, and the benefit of the value of the asset at the end of the term.

During the period of use, the rewards of ownership are likely to be the right of unrestricted use of the asset and the retention of the profits which result from its use. The lessee's risk will include losses due to the unsuitability, or unreliability, of the asset, and, therefore, if the lessor does not accept responsibility for the performance or the condition of the asset after delivery, this will suggest that the lease is of a finance nature.

The right to the major proportion of the sale proceeds will be one of the rewards of ownership, but it does infer a risk in so far as the residual value may be less than envisaged at the start. Under a hire agreement, the residual risk will remain firmly with the lessor at all times. Where there is a provision for the lessee to benefit from the larger share of the sale proceeds resulting from the sale of the asset, the lease is likely to be considered to be a finance lease.

It is unusual for a lessee of an asset to have exactly the same rights as an owner. Most leases will prohibit the lessee from disposing of the asset during the term of the lease and will require the return of the asset to the lessor at the end of the period of hire. Leases will frequently deny the lessee the right to modify the asset without the prior consent of the lessor. However, these types of restrictions will only be relevant in the classification of a lease in context with other matters. For instance, restrictions relating to the period during which the asset must be retained will not be relevant if the lease term corresponds closely to the period for which the lessee would have kept the asset if the lessee had bought it. Controls over modifications will not be relevant if it can be seen that the lessee would be unlikely to want to modify the asset.

The ninety per cent test

In cases of difficulty, SSAP 21 prescribes an arithmetic test to assist in the classification. This is known as the ninety per cent test. Under the test, a lease is presumed to be a finance lease if, at the outset, the present value of the minimum lease payments amounts to substantially all of the fair value of the asset, when the payments are discounted at the rate implicit in the lease. 'Substantially all' is generally taken to be 90 per cent or more of the fair value.

For the purposes of the test, a lease is considered as an exchange between two parties, under which the lessor parts with an asset in exchange for the payments required by the lease and an interest in the value of the asset at the end of the lease.

The lessor's interest in a finance lease will principally consist of the lease payments, and any interest in the residual value will be quite small. In the case of an operating lease, the residual value will be a far more important part of the lessor's interest.

The test demands that the minimum lease payments and the lessor's interest in the residual value are discounted at the rate implicit in the lease. The total of these payments (the present value) is compared with the fair value of the asset. If the result amounts to substantially all of the fair value (and therefore the lessor's interest in the residual value is very small), then it is to be presumed that the lease is a finance lease, in the absence of other evidence to the contrary.

The interest rate implicit in the lease

The ninety per cent test requires the payments to be discounted at the rate implicit in the lease. It is called this because at the start of the lease, the lessor has neither made a profit nor a loss. The excess over the amount the lessor has invested in the lease asset and the lessor's interest in the residual value represents a compensation for the delay in receipt of payments, analogous to a finance charge in a non-tax based product. The rate of return required by the lessor may therefore be taken to be the rate which discounts all of the future payments back to an amount equivalent to the value of the leased asset at the start of the lease.

The implicit rate can be calculated provided the lessee knows the minimum lease payments, the fair value of the leased asset and any unguaranteed residual value, the benefit of which accrues to the lessor.

Where the lessee does not have sufficient information, the rate must be estimated by reference to the rate which a lessee would expect to pay on a similar lease. The lessee's borrowing rate is unlikely to prove a suitable substitute. This is because of the inclusion of the benefit of the lessor's right to capital allowances which will have been included in the lease evaluation and will have the effect of reducing the cost of the lease rentals.

The effect of the test

As the residual value rises, then the implicit rate increases and the present value of the lease payments falls as a proportion of the fair value. When the residual value is nil, the lease payments represent 100 per cent of the fair value. It is therefore likely that increasing the residual value will increase the likelihood that a lease will be classified as an operating lease, because the lessee is not acquiring all of the risks and rewards of ownership.

The residual value and the present value of the lease payments will always add up to the fair value, due to the nature of the calculation. Thus, the amount attributable to the lease payments will be equal to, or will exceed, 90 per cent of the fair value only where the amount attributable to the residual value is equal to, or less, than 10 per cent. The ninety per cent test can therefore be performed simply by reference to the lessor's interest in the residual value (to the extent that it is not guaranteed by the lessee). If this is small, then the lease will usually be classified as a finance lease. Where the estimated residual value is less than 10 per cent of the fair value of the asset, then its present value must also be less than 10 per cent, and the lease may be classified as a finance lease.

Particular difficulties can occur when the lease payments reflect changes in the taxation conditions, or reflect grants available to the lessor. In such circumstances, classification will have to be based on whatever evidence is available.

The minimum lease payments

Only the minimum lease payments due by the lessee are to be included in the ninety per cent test. They are those payments which are taken to reimburse the lessor for the investment in the asset and for the cost of the finance in respect of it. They exclude any rentals which are contingent (such as additional mileage charges for motor vehicles) and any part of the rental which represents payment for services provided by the lessor and other expenses borne by the lessor.

All other payments required by the lease will be included in the minimum lease payments. Even if they are referred to as fees, all payments due at the beginning of the lease should be included.

Where the lessee guarantees the residual value of the asset, the amount of the guarantee should also be included, as it reflects the extent to which the lessee is interested in the residual value of the asset.

Common lease types

The usual classification of these common lease types is as follows:

1. *Leases of land and buildings*: Usually classified as operating leases as residual values are significant, and accrue to the lessor, who also enjoys a significant reward of ownership where rent reviews ensure the lessor obtains the benefit of increasing property values.

2. *Lease purchase (hire purchase) contracts*: Generally classified as finance leases, as they require the lessee to purchase the asset, or contain a purchase option bargain. If, however, a contract provided for the sale to the lessee at market value, and that value was relatively large, the contract could conceivably be described as an operating lease.

3. *Leases for office machinery*: Often classified in operating leases, as the term

is frequently significantly less than the working life. Most hirings will include maintenance and the rental will be increased accordingly.

4. *Vehicle leases*: Where the residual value accrues to the lessor without a guarantee from the lessee, generally classifed as operating leases, as with most contract hire contracts. Where the sale proceeds are passed to the lessee by way of a refund of rentals, then classification will be as a finance lease.

Accounting for finance leases

SSAP 21 requires that finance leases must be capitalised.

Ascertaining the initial value of the leased asset

Leases should first be recognised in the accounts on the earlier of the date the asset is brought into use, or the date from which the rentals first accrue. At the inception of a finance lease, there will be an asset and a liability of equal amounts. After inception, the asset and the liability will be accounted for separately and will rarely be shown at the same value.

SSAP 21 requires that the value placed on both the leased asset, and the obligation in respect of rental payments, at the point of lease inception should be the present value of the minimum lease payments, calculated at the rate implicit in the lease.

Where, as would normally be the case, the present value of the minimum lease payments amounts to substantially all of the fair market value of the asset, the fair market value may be substituted for the present value of the lease payments, in respect of both the asset and the lease obligation.

Accounting for the leased asset

An asset held under a finance lease should, in principle, be treated in the books of account just like any other asset. Depreciation should be charged so as to reduce its value to its estimated residual value at the end of its useful life. In accounting for the leased asset, the life used for depreciation should not exceed the lease term (including any renewal period). A residual value should only be placed on the asset if there is a reasonable probability that the lessee will receive the benefit of that residual value. This might occur by way of a refund of rentals amounting to a high proportion of sale proceeds, or by the release of a guarantee of a residual value included in the minimum lease payments.

Accounting for obligations and rentals under finance leases

Rentals paid under finance leases are considered to represent partly a payment to the lessor of the funds used in acquiring the asset, and partly the payment of a finance charge. The total amount of the finance charge may be easily calculated by subtracting the amount at which the lease was originally capitalised from the total minimum lease payments.

It is a requirement of SSAP 21, that the finance charge should be recognised in such a way as to give a constant rate of charge on the balance of the outstanding obligation. Where the rate implicit in the lease is known, or can be calculated, then applying it to the balance of the obligation will correctly determine the finance charge element for the period in question.

This method is known as the 'actuarial' method. It is a difficult method to apply without the aid of a computer and in such cases, resort to a simpler method may be appropriate, particularly where the level of finance charge is modest. Two methods are well known. These are the sum of digits method and the straight line method.

The sum of digits method is also known as the rule of 78, and with this method, the finance charge paid in each period is a fraction of the rental payable in each period, and this decreases progressively for each successive period.

It is first necessary to calculate the number of periods to which the finance charge relates. This will generally be the number of rental periods in the primary lease period, where rentals are payable in arrears, and one fewer where rentals are payable in advance. A quick method of calculating the total where there are a large number of periods is to apply the formula:

$$\frac{n(n + 1)}{2}$$

where n is the number of periods. This is dealt with in more detail under the section dealing with the computation of lease purchase charges.

The approximation of the sum of digits is only really satisfactory when the finance charges are modest. It is unlikely therefore to be suitable for longer leases extending beyond five years. The other disadvantage with the method is that it is difficult to adapt to leases with uneven rental profiles.

With the straight line method the finance charge is simply divided equally by the number of accounting periods, and then a constant amount is recognised within each period. This method is therefore only likely to be acceptable where the level of the finance charge is not material to the accounts in question.

The maturity of obligations under finance leases

The total amount of obligations under finance leases needs to be analysed by reference to the time of maturity, in order to derive the amounts required by the Companies Act and by SSAP 21. The amont of the obligation will be that element of the payments which falls due in an accounting period and which represents capital repayment excluding the finance charge.

Accounting for operating leases

An operating lease is a lease in which the lessee has less than 'substantially all' of the risks and rewards of ownership, and the accounting requirements are considerably less extensive than those of finance leases. The asset does not have to be recognised in the financial statements prepared by the lessee, and the rental payments are simply treated as revenue deductions in the profit and loss account. There will be no apportionment between capital repayments and finance charge. Any liability, which is included in the lessee's balance sheet, will only represent rental payments which have accrued at the balance sheet date.

It will be important for lessees to ensure that the requirements of SSAP 21 will be met by their policies and procedures. The total rental payable under an operating lease should be charged on a straight line basis (unless there is a specific reason why an alternative should be adopted), irrespective of the manner in which the lease calls for the payments. For instance, if a lease requires payments annually in arrears and the lessee pays £16,000 per year during the three years following the first, the rental stream will need to be respread in the accounts. Generally, the total rent of £48,000 should be spread over the four years at the rate of £12,000 per year. The cumulative rental expense will exceed the amount paid, and when this occurs the difference should be reflected in the balance sheet under accruals.

SSAP 21 requires that operating lease rentals be charged on a straight line basis, and it is therefore unlikely that there will be many exceptions when rentals are charged on a time basis. One example of an alternative treatment may occur where the ability of the asset to contribute towards profits deteriorates over the term of the lease. Amusement-with-prizes machines are a specific example, as their activity falls as users become bored with the activity. A further example may arise in the case of a computer installation, where the early part of the lease term may cover development and programming time rather than functional use, with the benefits of operation only accruing to the lessee at a later date.

Where rental payments are charged on some other basis, it may be that the payments will be more representative of the benefit derived from the asset than the amounts charged under the straight line method. This may occur when the rentals are linked to the operational use, or to market rates.

Where leases of land or buildings provide for regular rent reviews, it would comply with the spirit of the standard to charge the rentals payable up until the next rent review on a straight line basis. This treatment avoids the need to attempt to estimate the future level of rentals following review in order to spread the rentals on a straight line basis over the full term of the lease.

A premium is generally required when a lease for a building is acquired. This premium is usually capitalised in the accounts within the tangible fixed assets, and depreciated on a straight line basis over the shorter of the period of the lease, the period until the next rent review, or the useful life of the building. A straight line charge to the profit and loss account results and this will comply with SSAP 21 requirements. Under the standard it will still be acceptable to revalue leasehold land and buildings in accordance with market forces.

Disclosure requirements

SSAP 21 introduced important new disclosure requirements.

Assets held under finance leases

There is a choice of methods available under SSAP 21. Where leased assets are integrated with other fixed assets, the only information required is the net book value of the leased assets included in the total net book value and the depreciation charged in respect of the leased assets during the period.

Where the lessee holding several types of leased asset chooses to hold them together as a separate class of fixed asset, the gross amount (accumulated depreciation and depreciation charge for the period) in respect of each class of asset must be disclosed separately.

A more compact presentation is available to the lessee who integrates leased assets with other fixed assets, which may account for the popularity of this approach. Gross amount will usually be described as 'cost', a term which is reasonable to denote the value given to the asset based upon the present value of the obligations of the lessee incurred for the acquisition of the asset.

Obligations in respect of finance leases

The lessee's obligations regarding finance leases, together with an analysis of their dates of maturity are required by the standard. The analysis may either be of the amounts net of finance charge, or of the gross amounts. Obligations may be combined with similar items such as those for bank loan or overdrafts. Even when the obligations are combined, the net amount of the finance lease obligations must be disclosed separately. SSAP 21 allows for aggregate disclosure of the amounts falling due in more than one and less than five years.

Rental expense for operating leases should be disclosed between that relating to plant and machinery and that which relates to buildings or other expenses.

Commitments

SSAP 21 supplements existing requirements for disclosure in respect of finance and operating leases. Commitments should be disclosed where the lessee has entered into the lease at the balance sheet date, but its inception will occur at some later point.

For operating leases, the lessee will need to disclose the payment to which the lease commits the lessee during the following financial year. The payments should be analysed on the basis of the date on which the commitment will expire. Commitments for land and buildings will have to be separated from those of other operating leases.

When the leases are subject to rent reviews, the commitment to be reported will be that known to exist at the date of the balance sheet, but appropriate narrative must be added to avoid the possibility of confusion. If there is the possibility of a significant increase in the rental payments the narrative should clearly highlight it. Disclosure should also be made for contingent rentals, i.e. those which arise as a result of the use of the asset, or for dilapidations which may arise under the lease.

Source and application of funds statement

As the obligations in respect of finance leases appear in the balance sheet, they must also be dealt with in the funds flow statement. The movement of the obligation will often be most appropriately dealt with by showing increases (appertaining to new leases) as a source of funds, equal to the amount included in the application of funds, under the heading of the acquisition of leased fixed assets.

Decreases in the obligation, generally arising as a result of the capital payments made under the lease, should be shown as an application of funds. Where such a term is used in the funds flow statement, it will be appropriate to include obligations under finance leases.

The effect of lease capitalisation

The capitalisation of a finance lease does not affect the total expense of the lease recognised in the accounts over the full lease term. The effect of capitalisation upon the reported profits will depend on the term of the lease and the point in the period of the lease which has been reached.

Capitalising a lease which dictates regular payments of a fixed amount over the full life of the asset will generally result in an increase in the profit and loss charge in the accounting periods, and a reduction during later periods. Companies having an increasing leasing commitment will tend to report lower profits than would be the case were the leases not to have been capitalised in the manner prescribed by SSAP 21.

In the balance sheet, capitalisation will result in the recognition of an additional asset and an obligation. Upon lease inception these amounts will be equal. Shareholders' funds will therefore remain unaffected. The level of gearing will have increased.

Later in the lease term, the effect will be dependent upon the structure of the lease and its length in relation to the life of the leased asset. Companies having an increasing leasing commitment will tend to report a higher level of gearing than would be the case were the leases to be excluded from capitalisation.

Management accounts and SSAP 21

There is no requirement to introduce SSAP 21 into management accounting. However, many companies do prefer to draw up their internal affairs on the same basis as their statutory accounts.

The actuarial basis for capitalisation of leases may prove to be unduly time consuming for short periods required by internal accounts, and in the absence of a suitable spreadsheet or computer program some companies elect to use a straight light basis in the periodic management accounts.

However, when return on capital employed is used as a performance measure, capital employed may be redefined to include obligations under finance leases.

Taxation considerations after SSAP 21

The unprovided amounts which must be considered under the requirements of SSAP 21 will impact upon the taxation considerations of the balance sheet of the business. A part of the taxation consideration of both the lessee and the lessor has been studied earlier in this book. There is no substitute for independent professional advice in specific instances since no general book could help to tackle all the potential scenarios.

In tax law, the distinction between an operating lease and a finance lease is not relevant, but following the Inland Revenue Statement of Practice in April 1991, due cognisance must in future be paid to the Revenue approach to SSAP 21 companies. There is also the need to draw an important distinction between the leases where title remains vested in the lessor, and leases (generally of the nature of lease – or hire – purchase) where the passage of title to the lessee is permitted on performance of all the terms and conditions at the end of the lease term.

Lease (hire) purchase contracts

Under such a contract, the capital allowances relating to the asset are afforded to the lessee rather than to the lessor. The allowances are granted to the lessee with regard to the capital expenditure on the asset under the terms of the contract and, as discussed earlier, the asset is generally treated to have been acquired in the accounting period during which inception of the contract occurred.

The finance charge element will be allowed for tax purposes, but the capital element will not, since it will be subject to capital allowance computation.

Under SSAP 21, leases of this nature should be accounted for as finance leases, and the method of apportioning capital and finance charge out of the rental will normally be acceptable for tax purposes. As a result, the only differences in timing which occur will be analogous to that of other non-tax-based acquisitions (outright purchase, bank loan, etc.).

Finance leases (other than hire purchase)

Until recently, depreciation on a leased asset and the finance charges arising under the terms of a finance lease have not been allowed for tax purposes. The lessee would, however, usually expect to be able to deduct the rental charged under a lease agreement in deriving the taxable profit. The net effect would be to reduce the lessee's mainstream corporation tax liability on an accruals basis, when the rentals exceed the depreciation and the finance charge recorded in a particular accounting period. This would give rise to a potential deferred tax liability which would reverse over the period as the lease becomes reflected in the company accounts.

The Statement of Practice will, for SSAP 21 companies, as defined earlier, ultimately reduce the potential for a deferred tax liability arising in respect of finance lease timing differences.

Operating leases

In almost all cases the basis for recognition of lease payments under an operating lease will be the same for accounting and for tax treatment. This is because the basis upon which payments are made will generally be the basis for the rental expense (i.e. rentals are seen to accrue over a period of time).

In such cases, where an alternative method is applied (such as the straight line method) because it reflects the commercial benefit afforded by the transaction more accurately, this method may be considered by the Revenue in the assessment to taxation during the periods concerned. As a result, it is unlikely that material timing difference will occur in the consideration of operating leases.

Complex areas created by SSAP 21

There are areas which lead to possible difficulty and these include sale and leaseback transactions, leases with variation clauses, intra-group leasing and borrowing powers.

Sale and leaseback transactions

When a sale and leaseback occurs, the vendor passes good title to the lessor, but retains the use of the equipment under a lease which the vendor is granted by the lessor. Where the lease is a finance lease, the vendor retains substantially all of the risks and rewards of ownership, and may be seen to be in a similar position as if the vendor had borrowed the money. In other words, the vendor receives a sum of capital in return for the obligation to make payments over a period of time, and these sums will repay the capital sum together with the finance charges. The financing party receives a legal interest in the equipment.

However, where the leaseback is an operating lease, the vendor will no longer have substantially all the risks and rewards of ownership. Many companies in the retailing sector prefer to concentrate on their trading activities and not to devote their resources to capital acquisitions. Such companies will often prefer the vehicle of the operating lease.

In all kinds of sale and leaseback transactions, the tax considerations will be of great importance. The accounting difficulties with sale and leaseback transactions relate to the question of when the profit or loss on the sale should be recognised in the accounts of the vendor.

The sale and the terms of the lease will be negotiated concurrently, and the rental will be influenced by the amount of the sale proceeds rather than the market rental for the asset in question. In some cases it is even possible that the sale is not a genuine one, because there is no change in the economic ownership.

SSAP 21 restricts the recognition of apparent profits from sales which are followed by leasebacks. This is to ensure that transactions of this type are accounted for in relation to their commercial substance rather than their legal form. As a result, different rules will be applied depending upon whether the lease is a finance lease or an operating lease.

Specific attention should be given to the classification of sale and leaseback transactions. Evidence, such as the ninety per cent test, may not prove to be conclusive for a sale and leaseback transaction. One area to investigate should be the lease term in relation to the working life of the asset. If the term represents substantially all of the working life, the lease is likely to be an operating lease, whether or not the ninety per cent test is satisfied.

In general, it should be considered that the lessee has not disposed of substantially all of the risks and rewards of ownership, since the lessee will still have the use of the asset. The exceptions will arise when the lease is seen to be based upon a material residual for which the lessee is not required to give a guarantee, or when the rental is clearly a market rental.

Where the leaseback is an operating lease, then the vendor (lessee) no longer enjoys substantially all of the risks and rewards of ownership. SSAP 21 requires that the profits or losses arising from the transaction should normally be recognised immediately.

There are two exceptions where accounting should be deferred and amortised over the lease term. Where the lease is subject to rent reviews, amortisation should be made over the period until the next rent review. The exceptions are first, where the sale price exceeds the fair market value of the asset, in which event the excess of the sale price over the fair market value should be deferred, with any balance of profit being recognised immediately.

Second, where the sale occurs below market value and results in a loss which is compensated by rentals below market rate. In these circumstances, prudence should be used in assessing the amount of the loss which can be seen to be reflected in the rental payments and which should therefore be deferred.

There is no requirement under SSAP 21 that a particular method be used to calculate the amortisation. In most cases a straight line method will prove to be convenient and acceptable. However, where the difference between the sale proceeds and the fair value is substantial, consideration should be given to reflecting the finance-related nature of the amount involved by amortising on an actuarial basis.

Where the transaction results in a finance lease, then substantially all of the risks and rewards of ownership remain with the vendor. SSAP 21 prohibits the recognition of any profit or loss at the time of the transaction. Instead, any differences between the written down value of the asset and the sale proceeds will be deferred over the shorter of the term of the lease, or the useful life of the asset.

An exception may occur when the sale proceeds are materially less than the written down value, in which event, consideration should be given to whether the value of the asset brought forward was in excess of the asset's recoverable amount. If this is the case, then a provision for diminution should be made, and charged against the profit and loss account before the profit or loss relating to the sale is calculated.

There are two methods by which the leased asset and the obligation relating to a finance leaseback may be reflected in the financial statements. One is to treat the asset as if it were disposed of, and then to account for the lease in the manner required for any other lease. There may be some postponement of some of the profits and losses. This will result in the asset being carried forward at its approximate fair value at the time of the sale and leaseback, although this may be greater than its previous written down value, calculated by reference to historic value. The second approach is to leave the written down value of the asset undisturbed (apart from its reclassification as a leased asset), and then to recognise the full amount of the sale proceeds as a creditor. The rentals will then be apportioned between the repayment of this amount and a finance charge. This approach will often prove to be a fairer reflection of the substance of the transaction.

Although SSAP 21 fails to specify a method to be used to amortise deferred profits and losses, any deferred profit or loss should preferably be amortised using the basis for calculating depreciation of the asset. This will result in the net total of the depreciation and the amortisation of the profit or loss being the same as the depreciation charge on the written down value of the asset before the sale and leaseback.

Leases containing variation clauses

Many leases contain clauses which deal with variables which were assumed when the lease cashflow was evaluated. Such clauses are drafted in widely differing terms and the detail of specific wording will require careful study. The two most common variables relate to movements in interest rates and rates of corporation tax.

In some cases the lessee may assume all or part of the risk involved in connection with movements in interest rates. As a result, there will be provision for the rentals to be varied in accordance with specific circumstances, such as movement in a lending base rate. It will be necessary to use the best estimate of the rental payments due under the lease, based upon the circumstances known at the time, in arriving at the accounting treatment of the contract.

Theoretically, the calculation of the finance charges should be performed each time the rentals are varied, but in practice this will normally prove to be unnecessary. The difference between the actual rental payments and those which were assumed, will be dealt with by adjusting the finance charge recognised in each accounting period. The calculation may be simplified where there are several movements during an accounting period provided that the overall effect is not material. Only then will a full recalculation be likely to be necessary.

One of the main factors which the lessor will include in computing rentals will be the benefit of the deferral of tax liabilities through the availability of capital allowances. Most leases of substance will provide that the rentals will be adjusted to reflect changes in either the rate of corporation tax, or the rate of capital allowances. The wording, and therefore the impact, of such clauses will vary significantly. If the precise interpretation of such clauses is unclear, it will be necessary to make a prudent estimate of the adjusted rentals. Usually, the benefit of reductions will be realised by the lessee over the remaining term of the lease.

In the majority of situations, the preferred method of dealing with reductions will be to apply them to the future finance charges, rather than to make adjustments to the gross value of the asset acquired under the finance lease. This has the advantage that the profit or loss account will reflect the benefit of the reduction in rentals over the same period as the benefit is actually obtained. The apportionment of the revised finance charges will need to be recalculated.

In an extreme case, where the future rentals might amount to less than the net existing obligation, the obligation should be reduced by the total of the revised rentals. The excess will then be used to reduce the future depreciation charges. This will be best achieved by crediting the excess to accumulated depreciation. SSAP 21 does specifically exclude the recognition of a negative financing charge.

Intra-group leasing

Leases written between companies which are members of the same group must be accounted for on the same basis as for any other leases according to SSAP 21. No lease should be recorded in the group accounts, however, and appropriate adjustments must be made upon consolidation. This will eliminate the excess of the finance charges recognised by the lessor over those recognised by the lessee. The lessor's lease receivables should also be netted against the lessee's lease obligation.

To comply with the Companies Act, there should be separate disclosure of the amounts relating to finance leases which are due to, or from, a holding company, or fellow subsidiary, in the individual companies' accounts. Commitments due to, or from, subsidiaries should be included.

It will be the commercial nature of the leasing transaction, not simply the legal position of the parties to the contract which will determine the classification of the lease. Companies wishing to avoid the expense of capitalisation of intra-group leases will need to pay heed should they wish to structure such arrangements as operating leases.

Borrowing powers

There are many companies whose borrowing powers are restricted. Such restrictions may limit the total borrowings, or limit the ratio of borrowings to shareholders' funds.

As such restrictions vary considerably, their precise terms will require careful study to decide whether the capitalisation of leases will impact upon the future borrowing ability. However, it will evidently be desirable to ensure that descriptions in the statutory accounts recognise the legal differences between finance leases and borrowings.

CHAPTER 15

CURRENT DEVELOPMENTS

Introduction

There have been many illustrations throughout this book showing that government fiscal and administrative policy can have a large impact on the manner in which businesses favour a particular funding route. More succinctly, much of the growth in leasing during the 1970s was fuelled as a result of fiscal policy at the time. The taxation benefits, or otherwise, will frequently be a determining factor in the selection of a particular finance product in all except the smallest of transactions.

Taxation issues

Large value transactions

For some time large value lessors have believed that it is desirable to effect a mechanism, whereby prior clearance in respect of capital allowances could be obtained from the Inland Revenue before the lessor enters into a binding commitment to expenditure on the project. At the end of 1990, the Inland Revenue issued a public statement, which outlined arrangements for tax payers to be able to obtain guidance in respect of proposed contracts with complex tax implications. Although this proposal only appears to apply in certain circumstances, it does look as if it will go a long way towards satisfying the concerns of the major lessor companies.

Unusual assets

With the privatisation of the water supply industry in England and Wales at the end of 1989, some lessors have been approached by the new water companies seeking a leasing facility for the first time.

The nature of some of the equipment, being bespoke to the water industry, caused new questions to be raised concerning the lessor's right to capital allowances in respect of such equipment. The central tax district for the water companies has been of assistance to potential lessors of water company assets and has agreed to liaise with the parties to future contracts until some form of precedent is established.

Computer software

This area is one of the old chestnuts of the leasing industry which has grown in significance over the years, as the software element in computer installations has become more significant.

The Equipment Leasing Association (the trade body of the lessors) has suggested recently that it hopes to meet with representatives of the Inland Revenue, with the intention of securing the Revenue's agreement that licensed software subject to a lease agreement should qualify for writing down allowances claimed by the lessor.

VAT bad debt relief

The scope of relief for bad debts under VAT was extended under section 11 of the Finance Act 1990, bringing about some savings to lessors in respect of the VAT element of uncollected lease rentals.

The Budget of 1991 intimated that there was to be a reduction in the waiting period (from two years down to one year) before relief could be taken, which in turn will assist lessors in the future.

Taxation of company-owned private cars

There is growing concern on the part of the financiers, that the significant annual increases in the taxation scale charges relating to private use of company cars will impact upon their business in future.

It is likely that any further increases in such charges above the rate of inflation will cause company car drivers to elect to use their own car and to claim a mileage allowance from the employer. This will have an impact both upon the contract hire and rental industry and, ultimately, on the revenues of the Exchequer.

The matter is currently being addressed by representatives of the interested parties within the industry, namely, the British Vehicle Rental and Leasing Association, the Finance Houses Association and the Equipment Leasing Association. Meetings have been held between these representatives and members of the Inland Revenue's Personal and Business Taxation Department, during 1991.

The Associations' aims have been to see that the restriction of the deduction of the vehicle rental by the lessee, where the vehicle cost exceeds £8,000, should be removed. This potential loss of revenue would then be offset by a reduction in the rate of writing down allowance.

There have been other views expressed to the extent that future scale charges, in respect of private use of company-owned vehicles, should be computed under a system based upon the retail price of the car. At the present time, the charge is determined by reference to the size of the engine capacity and, where appropriate, the retail selling price of the vehicle.

Accounting issues

Accounting Standards

Under the Companies Act of 1989, a new statutory framework has been established. Formerly, the Accounting Standards Committee existed as a purely representative group, taking due account of the interests and proposals arising from the professional accountancy bodies. The Act replaced this Committee with the new Accounting Standards Board which reports to the Financial Reporting Council, whose responsibility it has now become to research and incept future accounting standards.

Although outside the scope of this book, it is of interest to note that there are moves afoot to bring about the future harmonisation of banking legislation within the EC member states. This will introduce many factors which will be of interest to the lessor and to the asset financier. Indeed, under pressure from international stock market interests, it is possible to foresee the day when a worldwide harmonisation of accounting standards is required.

While the United Kingdom has moved some distance towards the capitalisation of leases in the balance sheet, UK law continues to treat the leased asset separately. In many other countries of the world, the legal and taxation position is much more closely tied to the accounting treatment. The potential changes to taxation which could occur with global harmonisation are therefore of concern to any major national organisation.

Income recognition by lessors

From the point of view of the lessor, there is perhaps still too much latitude under SSAP 21 when it comes to the subject of income recognition by the lessor. It appears to be accepted at present that where the lessor moves away from the generally accepted accounting standards, profit takeout should never be recorded in the early years of a lease in such a manner that a loss will arise in later years.

The Equipment Leasing Association has recently taken steps to advise its membership of the importance of a consistent approach to income recognition.

Accounting for residual values

Residual values are of significance in operating leases, and because of the flexibility permitted under SSAP 21, they have caused difficulties in lessor accounting since the mid-1980s.

One of the greatest areas of difficulty to come to the fore during the current recession is the problem faced by the lessor in assessing the residual value to be placed on the leased asset at the inception of the lease. This is compounded by the decision of how the residual should be brought into account, by either the lessor, or some other party who has entered into a contract to assume the residual value risk.

In 1987, a joint working party was established between the Institute of Chartered Accountants in England and Wales and the Equipment Leasing Association. This body disbanded without producing firm proposals because it was believed at the time that the then UK Accounting Standards Committee would itself address the issues involved.

The latest initiative in this area has been the formation of a research group at the University of Lancaster. It has started working on a paper on residual value accounting for presentation to the Institute of Chartered Accountants in England and Wales. The Equipment Leasing Association has welcomed this Lancaster study and indicated its full agreement, and has offered its assistance with identifying the need for a new accounting standard on residual values in leasing.

Legal issues

The consumer credit legislation

As stated in earlier chapters, finance agreements with the unincorporated business and the partnership (professional or otherwise) will fall within the

Consumer Credit Act 1974 legislation when the balance financed is £15,000 or less, or the lease rentals (inclusive of VAT at the current rate on inception of the contract) are £15,000 or less.

The Department of Trade and Industry has stated its intention to remove the business user from the consumer credit legislation. In the absence of some definitive date when this is to occur, some work is currently being done on a Private Members Bill, in the hope of encouraging this change when the Act is amended to implement recent proposals regarding credit marketing.

Proposals by the European Commission

The European Commission has published proposals for a Directive on general product safety which could have an impact upon the business of the asset financier. Lessors, in particular, could become entangled with the role of the supplier, where they have either provided second-hand goods or acted as the importer of any goods. In current UK law there is a distinction between the lessor and the actual supplier, responsibility in respect of the safety of the goods remaining with the latter.

The position of the lessor in the UK is probably unique, and it will be necessary to put forward some argument which excludes the providers of finance in the definition of a 'supplier', if there are to be no unequal conditions in the internal European market for financial services.

The second proposal of importance to the asset financier issued by the European Commission concerns a new Directive with regard to defective services. This could affect those financiers who supply services in conjunction with the supply of goods. Under English law, the burden of proof that negligence has occurred remains with the individual who has suffered damage. However, the proposals for the European Commission Directive would have the reverse effect, so that it would be for the suppliers of the services to prove that their negligence had not occurred. It is generally believed that it is not the intention to include financial services, but careful attention to the future drafting of the Directive will be required from the financiers' representative bodies.

The draft of the Directive on consolidated supervision, issued by the European Commission, is under consideration by the Council of Ministers. The current differing level and scope of banking supervision within EC member states will, inevitably, cause some headaches for the asset financier. In some states, banking supervision is aimed at the assets side of the balance sheet, and leasing companies may become subject to regulation as a result of the nature of their credit business.

While the Second Banking Coordination Directive provides a blueprint for banking services in the single market, it does so on the basis of the principle of home state control of banking activities (of which finance leasing is one). UK leasing companies which are in the banking sector, and the leasing business which comes within the remit of the UK banking system, will be able to conduct leasing business in other EC states under their own home state supervision.

This will not necessarily be the case for the other lessors, and, even though they may not be able to obtain access to all states in the single market, they may still be subject to some home state regulation because of the nature of their credit business. This anomaly is generally regarded as a failure of the single market to provide access to these markets after 1992. Their position has been the subject of discussion with the Bank of England. However, the Bank appears unwilling to supervise leasing companies and, so far, there has been no decision in principle regarding the possibility of a Directive aimed specifically at clarifying the position of leasing and its supervision after 1992.

Summary

In common with most other industries, the asset finance industry is suffering from the downturn in the present economy. Future fiscal policy regarding company cars, the opportunities arising from the single market and the probability of inflation stabilising for a period at a much lower rate than in recent years, will all have an impact in the future. The trade associations will continue to play a vital part in the continuing development of asset finance products and the accompanying legislation.

The future of the industry is encouraging and the next chapter will look at some of the possible areas of activity.

CHAPTER 16

THE FUTURE OF THE ASSET FINANCE INDUSTRY

Introduction

At the time of writing this book, the London Business School, among other commentators, is predicting a prolonged period of high unemployment and weak investment. It is expected that there will be no real growth in personal incomes for the duration of 1991 and well into 1992. Hopes for an upturn in consumer demand will be based upon confidence in the retail marketplace. That confidence is unlikely to return while many thousands of people see redundancy as a very real threat.

The early indications are that the modest recovery in activity seen in the spring of 1991 has not been maintained and that the upturn will come later, and to a lesser extent, than was believed at the start of 1991.

The British economy is adjusting to Britain's membership of the Exchange Rate Mechanism (ERM) and the fact that an inflation rate of around 4 per cent a year should be sustainable in the future. Unemployment seems set to rise to around 2.8 million by the summer of 1992, and the prospects of a significant fall in numbers appears unlikely before the middle of the decade.

The outlook for commercial investment shows little to encourage the analyst. The cutbacks in production of 1991, which look set to be in the order of 16 per cent overall, appear unlikely to recover during 1992, with some commentators suggesting a further decline by some 3 or 4 per cent. Predictions have been made that gross domestic product (GDP) will fall by some 2 per cent during 1991, and the Confederation of British Industry (CBI) has reported that the uncertainty created by rising unemployment has offset the impact of lower interest rates on consumer demand.

Competition in the marketplace

Traditionally the clearing banks represented the first resort for the established borrower. The level of competition has increased substantially during recent years as 1992, the year of European political and monetary union, draws near. There have been several major new entrants to the British financial market and established financial institutions, such as the building societies, have been given a new freedom to expand their activities.

In volume terms the building societies have shown a substantial rate of growth in their personal lending, but the effect on profit has been undermined by the record number of repossessions that are finding their way on to an already depressed property market.

Finance companies are wrestling with an increasing level of default in virtually every portfolio other than large value funding. During 1991, a large part of their resource will be diverted into increased customer care activity, in an attempt to stem the flow of losses resulting from company failures.

Clearing banks, too, have similar difficulties, although some are perceived to have experienced problems from their large value borrowers as well as their less well known customers. Provision for potential bad debt will continue to increase during the second half of 1991, and it will not be until well into 1992 that it will be seen whether provisions have been unduly pessimistic.

On the edge of the current activity there are some major names whose management seem set to address the market with vigour next year. It is significant to note that G.E. Capital Corporation acquired some of the retail branch network of Mercantile Credit in July 1991. G.E. Capital is one of the major players in the operating lease market in the United States and appears to view Europe as a rich market for development in the future. The company has maintained an active, though limited, marketing stance in the corporate sector in the United Kingdom, for the last four years or so. With its acquisition of the Mercantile Credit portfolio from Barclays and other operating lease activities, it will be poised to further increase its activity from an established network and with experienced staff. Without the problems of serious default to contend with, G.E. looks very well placed to capitalise on its position when the United Kingdom begins to move out of recession.

The recent background to the industry

The 1970s

In the mid-1970s, the clearing banks acquired a number of major finance companies whose management and staff had developed an expertise in marketing both tax-based and non-tax-based funding products. The Finance Act of 1972 had introduced first year capital allowances at a rate of 100 per cent on most types of plant and equipment. By putting together this expertise, the tax advantages and the financial resources of the banks, all of which were generating significant profits charged at a mainstream rate of 52 per cent, leasing activity made giant inroads into the marketplace.

The timing was right. The banks had adequate taxable capacity and financial resources to make further advances within Bank of England controls relating to eligible liabilities. The customer base was generally non-tax paying due to stock relief provisions and therefore unable to benefit from the higher rate of capital allowances. By building the benefit of the capital allowances relieved at a mainstream rate of 52 per cent into the lease pricing, the banks were able, through their finance subsidiaries, to generate significant earnings through a facility which was highly acceptable to the customer.

The 1980s

By the start of the 1980s, the government had recognised that the acceleration of capital allowances had generated a climate in which many businesses were acquiring assets with a view to tax deferment, rather than for their immediate application in the business for which they were acquired. In the 1984 Finance Act, a general scaling down of allowances was announced, with the effect that the capital allowances in respect of most types of plant and equipment would be claimed at a rate of 25 per cent per annum on a reducing balance basis.

Some financial commentators predicted that this would spell the end of the leasing era, because of the removal of many of the fiscal benefits accruing to the product. This was not to be the case, leasing had become generally accepted as a structured means of acquiring equipment. This view, coupled with the impending change in accounting requirements relating to the treatment of leased assets as 'on balance sheet' items, helped to maintain leasing products as a major method of funding for industry.

Although the fiscal benefits were deferred with the effect of reducing margins, the increased volumes which were generated and increased expertise in funding structures using SWAPS maintained leasing as a profitable product in the financier's portfolio. It was a product which could be introduced to businesses not otherwise customers of the clearing bank, opening the doors for other dialogue.

However, increased competition and the start of a recession in the consumer marketplace at the end of the decade caused senior managers to reappraise their investment in their finance subsidiaries, the majority of which had heavy investments in the retail market in addition to their corporate portfolios.

The present

By the start of 1991, several of the leading banks had announced their intention to divest themselves of their retail operations in the finance sector. This would, ultimately, result in a significant reduction in the cost base and a reduction in staffing levels, accommodated by a mixture of redundancy and early retirement.

For the first time in several years, the banks were faced with the responsibility of reporting significant customer repayment problems. This had arisen, not as a result of the 'Third World' debt crisis, but as a direct result of recession in the UK sector. There was a need to define the remedies which were to be taken, and a principal focus has generally been to address the peripheral activities, such as the finance subsidiaries.

Whether this is the right long-term strategy remains to be seen. Senior managers in the major banking groups are currently rewarded by profit-related pay, and the need to address current issues by relatively short-term methods will clearly be in the interest of the individual, in order to maximise the earnings potential. However, it is not the purpose of this book to comment specifically on any particular marketing design.

The future for the products of the asset finance industry

Leasing is an established vehicle of finance. Its attraction remains its flexibility both in terms of cashflow and the effect which it can be designed to have on the shape of the balance sheet. The product is a useful marketing weapon in the armoury of the banking group. Customers have far less allegiance to the lessor than they do to the clearing banker, a fact which can be deployed as an effective means of entry into a new customer.

Hire purchase, now often marketed in the style of lease purchase, is a long standing and traditional method of acquisition, free from many of the security requirements currently placed upon a bank loan.

For reasons of flexibility, and the manner in which the customer can avoid too great a dependence on one funding source, it is difficult to envisage a situation in which either leasing or hire purchase will decline significantly in their popularity, unless Government legislation were to bring about some major disadvantage.

The loan will continue to be important in cases where security is available and the magnitude of the project justifies the overall cost.

Future marketing activity in the asset finance industry

Small ticket transactions

The cost justification of future activity will be a prime consideration to the financier. The increasing costs relating to staff (one of the financier's largest outlays) will influence the manner in which smaller transactions are handled.

There are three possible routes through which the financier can handle low value transactions and these are the following:

1. Telephone sales.
2. Use of bank premises.
3. Third party introductions.

With telephone sales the financier can employ permanent internal staff to conduct sales through the telephone using the postal services to deliver documentation. If campaigns are conducted effectively, calls can be programmed to establish contact with the customer at the most opportune time when the purchase is under consideration. Adequate training is vital for personnel.

The disadvantages are minimal if the structure is well planned. However, uncoordinated activity may result in very high marketing costs in relation to the volume of business written. In addition, there is a relatively high entry cost in establishing an accurate database, although most major financiers will have a wide base of customers and prospects within their existing systems.

Staff will benefit as the role of telesales may be the most suitable entry point for the young and inexperienced salesperson from where a career in finance may be built.

As either an alternative to, or as an addition to, a telephone sales activity, the finance subsidiary may elect to locate members of its sales staff within the business centres of its parent bank. In this way it will be possible for the resident staff member to seek business from within that geographical location, while travelling costs are kept to a minimum.

There may be some disadvantage to the financier in so far as direct control will, at least in part, be subordinated to an alternative line management, with a potential threat to team building and morale. Choice of staff will be important in considering this as an alternative, because it is likely they will be called upon to work on their own initiative more than would be the case if they were to be located in a traditional branch office.

Typically, third party introductions will arise from some form of formal sales-aid relationship with a manufacturer or supplier, usually known by the financier as the dealer. The relationship with the large dealer will often be negotiated at a national level, with service from the financier taking the form of training and document processing being handled through local offices.

The financier will benefit considerably from the introduction to a volume of business with a cross-section of customers, while having minimal marketing costs compared to the circumstances had the financier had to seek out the business from scratch. Additionally, the customers acquired from this route will be available to the financier for additional promotions at a later date.

The principal risk to the financier will be the manner in which the financial services are introduced by the dealer's sales force. Training and local relationships will become an important factor in the control which the financier will wish to exercise over the way sales are accommodated and the facilities presented.

Although sales-aid originated as a way of handling high volume, low value transactions, it has been developed to the point where transactions involving tens of thousands of pounds worth of equipment, such as contractors' plant and machine tools, can be accommodated swiftly and efficiently.

It is a particularly beneficial facility for the dealer when the market falls into recession, since it represents an effective method of overcoming the customer's price objections. The cost to which the customer objects can be spread over such a period as would seem to be prudent in the light of the working life of the asset in the customer's hands. The dealer can also assist the customer with balance sheet planning by introducing a leasing package to the deal.

For all of these reasons, it seems most likely that sales-aid finance will be set for a period of growth while the economy remains in its depressed state.

Middle and large ticket transactions

Middle and large value transactions will continue to arise from established relationships, and the financier currently has an opportunity to concentrate on relationship building in order to benefit when the market begins to recover.

When sales fall away in a recessionary period, most business managers will revise their budgeted capital expenditure. The experienced financier recognises that, for a large organisation, such reduction in expenditure merely represents a moratorium, and that replacement equipment will be needed in greater volume once the period of austerity comes to an end. Time spent in building a rapport with the established prospective customer will never be wasted in the longer term.

There is, at the time of writing this book, evidence that even the largest organisations have reviewed their expenditure plans. It is perhaps unrealistic to suggest that there will be any major change in this position at least until the second half of 1992. From the finance lessor's point of view this may be quite opportune, since there have been recent reports that several major lessor groups are currently in the position of having limited tax shelter.

Nevertheless, the experienced finance executives will be busy. They will be concentrating effort on developing a mutual understanding of future needs with the management of the larger business, so that, when the upturn in the economy does come, they will be best placed to take advantage of it. A good salesperson recognises that selling is an art form, and, like any art form, the quality of the final result depends upon the amount of preparation put into achieving it. However, it seems most likely that it will be at least another twelve months before the middle ticket market sector shows material signs of recovery in capital expenditure.

Specialist activities

April 1990 saw the collapse of Atlantic Computer Systems plc, a major company which specialised in the area of computer leasing. Atlantic had written leases with the option for the lessee to upgrade the computer installation at predefined dates within the lease term. Under some contracts, the lessee could even terminate without replacement at certain times during the overall term of the extended lease agreement.

These options were attractive to the lessees, but proved to be unworkable, and when Atlantic could not honour its contracts, an Administrator was appointed. The situation has now been at least partially resolved by IBM UK Financial Services which has now offered substitute agreements to lessees. Nevertheless, the event has strengthened the call by interested parties to establish appropriate accounting standards in respect of residual values in computer leasing, the absence of which seems to have been at the root of the troubles within Atlantic.

Despite these developments, the activity of computer leasing is probably one of the strongest areas for future long-term growth in the leasing portfolio. It is to be hoped that the Inland Revenue will issue a statement concerning the lessor's entitlement to allowances in respect of licensed software, now that this element of a system's cost is becoming much greater.

As suggested in the previous chapter, there is growing concern, particularly among vehicle hire and rental operators, regarding the rapidly increasing scale charges for private use of a company-owned car. The operators fear that any further increase above the rate of inflation will cause the employee to favour the option of using a private vehicle and then charging the employer for its use on a mileage basis. If this prediction comes true, it will have serious ramifications for the corporate financier, since cars represented by far the largest category of assets purchased by member companies, according to the figures published for 1990 by the Equipment Leasing Association.

The contract car hire operator has adopted a market stance of offering the customer the freedom to build a funding package tailored to the requirements of the business at a competitive price. There have been massive investments in technology, with computer systems being able to analyse all areas of the operating costs of a fleet. However, little, if any, of this investment will be of significance to the employee who when looking at the tax coding slip feels that just that bit too much is being lost for the benefit of the private use of a company Ford Sierra.

If there is a general return to the use of privately owned vehicles, the Exchequer would notice a significant decline in its revenues from personal taxation over a period of time. The motor manufacturing industry would also suffer from further shortfalls in the order books, as the majority of private purchasers appear to keep their vehicles longer than do the fleet operators.

The future of customer service

Customer service will be of paramount importance to the retention of customers as competition increases. It is generally considered to be easier and cheaper to convert an existing customer to accept an additional product, than it is to sell to a new customer. The possible downside to this philosophy is that research indicates that the existing customer is more likely to expect discounts from the financier.

The finance market is moving towards a position where it wishes to be seen to be willing to give more advice than has been the tradition in the past. There is a risk in so far as the financier may become liable for the results of the advice given, and a closer involvement with the professions in handling customers' requirements will probably come about.

Central processing units (groups of people working in one, fairly large, administrative base) are now quite common in the retail finance sector, and it would not be surprising to see moves in this direction in the corporate sector during the next few years. There are cost savings available to the financier, and greater control and consistency in handling high volumes of business are all possible. With the present advances in communications technology, it is now practical to have a sales office serviced by an administration team based two hundred miles away, without detriment to the level, or quality, of customer service.

The future of computerisation

Manual record cards and filing systems in the sales offices are giving way to computer-based systems as the cost of portable computers and local area networks fall. Investment in technology, at least in theory, should increase productivity, while speeding up market analysis, and encouraging greater efficiency in the use of resources for business development. However, there will be a need for thorough training of personnel at all levels if technology is to be used to maximum effect.

Fewer people will be required to handle larger volumes of work, and the dependence on branch offices is likely to decline. Those centres which remain will be for customer contact (sales offices) where all of the financier's services may be discussed with specialists who have been trained in specific areas of the financier's business.

Investment in technology will allow the creation of national, or regional, administration and processing centres, reducing the dependence on a large and expensive head office base. However, security procedures will need to be reviewed constantly because the new technology opens up new gateways for unauthorised access by the intruder or the disillusioned ex-employee.

Risk assessment systems will be developed to speed the process of credit approval by automating much of the analytical process which goes into preparing a new business submission.

Risk management in the future

The financier of the future will need to assess transactions as a whole, and technology will be used to speed up the process, while also providing the senior management with up-to-date and meaningful management information to give a competitive edge. The financier will have areas of risk, both in the business on the books, and in the way in which it is funded.

Ratio analysis

The use of ratios in the analytical process has been fundamental to credit assessment for many years. There are already many software packages from which the customer's accounts can be analysed into significant ratios. These can be run on the single personal computer, the network or on the mainframe.

The principal benefit will be derived from the speed of the process and the level of accuracy which a practised operator can bring to the process. A possible disadvantage could be that the person writing the report does not appraise the content as thoroughly as would be the case if the analysis was conducted manually. However this will be a matter for the training of the financier's risk assessment personnel and is not a limitation to technology in the business.

Cash, working capital and funds flow analysis

These analytical tools will all form a greater part of the credit vetting process in the larger transaction. The dynamics of a balance sheet for a particular industry, in a geographic location, have yet to be fully recognised as an historic performance measurement by many financiers and even by some banking groups.

There will need to be a recognition for the sake of the financier's shareholders at least, that, having regard to the differences in size of the businesses within an industry, the balance sheet of companies operating within the same market sector will be similar.

A classically quoted example is that of the supermarket chain, operating on a 'cash positive' basis, with very few debtors and little or no term borrowings (unless these arise from joint venture operations away from the mainstream activities). Conversely, a heavy engineering company will have a tendency towards long-term borrowings, but will also maintain seasonal overdrafts supporting stock and working capital needs throughout the trading year.

The skilled analyst will be able to build computer-based models of the balance sheet dynamics of a particular market for comparison with specific customer profiles. This might not in itself assist the credit vetting process, but it will pinpoint the questions which should be settled before future funds are advanced.

Computerisation will help in future cashflow analysis and to ascertain for how long a business can sustain its present rate of growth without recourse to future borrowing – i.e. the sustainable growth rate.

In the present climate, there can be few financiers who are not currently reappraising their credit vetting techniques with a view to bringing about an improvement in their debt underwriting techniques.

However, what is certain is that there will never be any substitute for a clear established working relationship between the financier and the client. Computers can only assist in the process. Today it might be thought to be inconceivable that they will be capable of reaching conclusions in larger transactions, but who knows what is around the corner?

Treasury and taxation management

Both of these areas have already been addressed by the clearing banks. Systems exist to evaluate the risks and rewards of a transaction from both the taxation and the funding viewpoints.

It is now possible for the corporate treasurer to move large sums globally to or from foreign subsidiaries using technology in the office. Major banks offer 'on-line' facilities to their dealing rooms from the terminal in the customer's office. Electronic banking is a firmly established concept in the major organisations and is seen as an area for considerable growth and development in other sectors during the remainder of this decade. It will continue as a fee earning service of the financier.

Residual value risk

This area is ripe for exploitation by the software houses. Assessment of an asset's potential residual value at the end of a period of defined economic use, and given a set of economic circumstances at the time of disposal, is something the asset financier would pay dearly to be able to do.

Vehicle operators, both commercial and motor car, are reasonably adept and have developed their own systems. Many suppliers have maintained detailed records for years, but the UK asset finance industry has been lamentably slow at using the information which exists.

Senior managers will of course need to be able to interpret the data they receive, since the data will only be of historic value, but this will represent a giant leap forward in the risk assessment of the great majority when it occurs.

Summary

The current economic outlook in the short term is bleak. Motor vehicle dealers are selling cars at near cost price and hoteliers face severely reduced occupancy. Poor consumer confidence has impacted on the market with many businesses suffering poor liquidity and increasing bad debts. Manufacturing output is severely down. The pressures on the finance sector are as great as they have ever been, and as larger numbers of institutions compete for a diminishing slice of the cake, margins are likely to fall.

The single European market of 1992 does not seem to have sparked off enthusiasm from the UK financiers. This is hardly surprising because, excepting the mainstream banks, most have structured themselves to accommodate only the needs of the domstic marketplace. However, the recent announcement by Lombard North Central stating that it has established a UK joint venture with Transamerica Leasing (the US freight container and trailer leasing company) to offer operating leases on truck trailers is an interesting development.

Whether the effects of 1992 will bring any surprises by the middle of the 1990s remains to be seen. Meanwhile, the asset finance industry will have plenty with which to occupy itself as a result of the recession of the early 1990s.

Costs will continue to be cut and the medium term result is likely to be a smaller number of offices, connected by advanced computer systems, handling a wider range of financial and insurance-based products. Fee income is an area which the financier can be expected to promote more actively as a measure to make up for falling margins, and attempts will be made to rebuild margins based on quality of service and investment in training and technology.

Internally, there will be moves in the banking groups to increase the numbers of the financier's staff who are contracted to work on a reward-related pay system, reflecting more accurately their personal contribution to the business. This will represent progress towards the standards applied outside the subsidiaries of the mainstream clearers, in an attempt to focus reward away from the annual review which has traditionally reflected overall group progress and the rate of inflation.

Thus, by the middle of the 1990s we can expect to see a leaner, fitter finance industry, one in which effort is rewarded more directly to result.

However, it will be some time after the end of the current recession before the effect of the bad debt position is removed from the financiers' balance sheets, and the industry is ready to accept the challenges and opportunities afforded by the economic and monetary union of 1992. Meanwhile, the door will be open to increasing competition and both the French and the German financiers look well placed to accept the challenge.

GLOSSARY

Accrual accounting: A method of apportioning finance payments to the periods to which they relate.

For example, a business pays a rental of £1,800 quarterly in advance on 1 June 1991. The year-end of the company is 30 June. The rental will be apportioned as follows:

30 days to 30 June 1991, included in that year's accounts = £593.41

Remaining rental charged against profits in the year ended 30 June 1992 = £1,206.59

Acid test: Also known as the liquid ratio, this is the relationship between the most easily realisable assets of a business, i.e.

$$\frac{\text{current assets (less stock)}}{\text{current liabilities}}$$

Actuarial method: A mathematically correct method of allocating finance charges at a constant rate on a given balance. Finance charges are calculated on a strict reducing balance basis and the proportion of the finance charge decreases with each rental that is made. Application of this method in accounting for rentals will have the effect of producing a constant rate of return on the net investment in the leased asset made by the financier.

Agency Purchase: An agreement wherein the financier agrees that the customer will act as the financier's agent for the purposes of acquiring assets which will then become the subject of financial contracts between the financier and the customer.

Associated company: A company is an associate of another, if one of the two has control of the other, or if both are under the control of the same person, or persons.

Bad debt relief: Generally, deduction of bad debts from profits in the tax computation will only be permitted in respect of specific, i.e. named debtors, proven to be bad, or to the extent that they may be estimated to be bad. There is a concession for hire purchase financiers operating in purely consumer fields, where a percentage of the total value of the hire purchase book may be used instead.

Balance sheet dynamics: The comparative study of the balance sheet of a business with the balance sheets of other organisations in a particular market sector.

Bargain: Describes the terms which may be contained in leases under which the lessee has the right or obligation to renew the lease or to purchase the asset on terms which are so favourable that it is reasonable to assume that the lessee will exercise that right. Leases are generally accounted for on such a basis.

Block discounting: A method used to finance instalment credit book debts which involves the sale of the finance agreement at a discount. It is used by dealers as a means to release the capital tied up, thereby allowing for an expansion of additional business.

Borrowing interval: A ratio to highlight the relationship between the working capital of a business and its sales.

Capital allowances: The owner of equipment is allowed to deduct a percentage of the cost of an asset from his or her corporation tax liability in each year that the asset is retained for use in the business.

Historically, the rates of allowance available in the year of acquisition for plant and equipment, or commercial vehicles have been the following:

For expenditure incurred on or after 22 March 1972 – 100 per cent
For expenditure incurred on or after 14 March 1984 – 75 per cent
For expenditure incurred on or after 1 April 1985 – 50 per cent
For expenditure incurred on or after 1 April 1986 – nil

From 1 April 1986, a writing down allowance at a rate of 25 per cent per annum on a reducing balance basis has been given. There are provisions to accelerate the rate of write-off for tax purposes in respect of assets which are to be retained for use in the business for less than five years.

Capital expenses: Costs which relate to items which should be included within the balance sheet and which relate to the acquisition of plant and machinery, or, generally, improvements to buildings. Such expenses will usually be capitalised and then become the subject of a claim for capital allowances.

Capital lease: A term used in the US standard on accounting for leases (FAS 13) to describe a finance lease.

Capital reserves: These can arise in several ways, but the most common is when the fixed assets are revalued. The reserve then represents the excess over the book value. Capital reserves form part of the shareholders' funds and are only distributable under an order of the court.

Cash accounting: A method of accounting for finance payments on the basis of the date when they fall due and payable, rather than the period to which they relate.

Cashflow: This is the term which refers to money going into or out of a business during a period of account.

Cash going into a business can arise from sources such as cash from operations (profit plus depreciation added back), increases in borrowings, the sale of fixed assets, or share issues.

Cash outflows from a business can include items such as the payment of dividends, taxation, or sums due on the purchase of fixed assets, together with loan repayments made.

Charges: There are two types of charge. A floating charge allows the company to deal freely with its assets and will always be enforceable after a fixed charge. The exception occurs where the floating charge prohibits a loan with prior rights on the security of fixed assets and the lender under the fixed charge was aware of it.

Connected party: In the terms of a leasing contract, disposal of the leased equipment to a party connected with the lessee may prejudice the right to the claim for capital allowances. Connected parties can include the immediate relations of the owners of a business, including their parents, and their children, or husband or wife, where they acquire the leased asset in a personal capacity.

Contingent liability: This is a potential liability in the future. For example a contingent liability arises when one party guarantees another. The liability under the guarantee crystallises when the borrower defaults.

Contingent rentals: Rentals, the amount of which varies as a result of factors other than the simple passage of time. They may be dependent upon the hours of operation or the amount of use to which the asset is put.

Corporation tax: The tax levied on the profits of companies. There are three bands and these are defined by the level of profit generated in each accounting period, as follows:

1. The small companies' rate: a lower rate of tax is applied to businesses whose profits do not exceed a defined level.
2. The mainstream rate: this is the standard rate of corporation tax and will be higher than the small companies' rate.
3. The marginal rate: this allows for the catching up necessary in order that all of a company's profits above the level set for the mainstream rate are charged to taxation at the mainstream rate. The marginal rate will be higher than the small companies' rate and the mainstream rate. Every £1 of profit above the maximum level set for the small companies' rate and below the level set for the mainstream rate will be charged to taxation at the marginal rate.

The Inland Revenue Statement of Practice SP1/91 requires an election to be made if profits are to be charged at the small companies' or the marginal rates.

Cost of sales: This is made up of the manufacturing and selling costs of a business and it is deducted from the turnover to calculate the gross profit.

Credit given: The number of days which a business allows its debtors (customers) before payment has to be made.

Credit taken: The number of days which a company takes before it pays its creditors.

Creditors: These are accounts for the supply of goods or services which are due for payment within the next twelve months.

Current assets: Assets such as stock and debtors which are likely to be converted into cash within twelve months. Cash in hand or in the bank will be shown under current assets.

Current Liabilities: This category will include items such as creditors, bank overdrafts and taxation, which fall due for settlement within the next twelve months.

Debentures: These are legally enforceable debts, as distinct from the capital of the company. The debenture is a document given to the debenture holder by the company and the debenture holder becomes a creditor of the company.

De-pooling: Short life assets, during the term of the election, and expensive motor cars are kept in a separate account (pool) for the purposes of computing capital allowances. This is in order that the tax written-down value can be compared with the proceeds of disposal, and the process is often referred to as de-pooling.

Depreciation: This is a charge which is deducted from profits representing the wearing out of an asset over a period. Plant, machinery and vehicles are usually depreciated whilst freehold land and buildings will often not be.

Dividend: The shareholders' return for their investment in the share capital of a business.

Dividend cover: The number of times that the dividend can be divided into the post-tax profit.

Dual rate of return method: A modification of discounted cashflow analysis where the cashflows of a project produce a surplus in some periods and a deficit in other periods.

Economic ownership: Under the terms of a finance lease, the lessee (or user of the equipment) effectively enjoys all the risks and rewards resulting from the use of the asset. It is comparable to his or her actual ownership. In economic terms (rather than in the terms of the law), the customer is viewed as having effective ownership.

Equal instalments method: A method of calculating the element of finance charge within each rental. The finance charge is regarded as accruing evenly over the full term of the agreement. Each rental is seen to contain an equal amount of capital and finance charge. The method is used mainly by dealers and has proved unpopular with financiers since it is not particularly accurate.

Equity: A part of the issued capital of a business and often used as an alternative description to the shareholders' interest.

Facility letter: A letter which documents the limits placed on the facility which the financier is willing to grant to the customer. The letter will generally state the security which may be required before funds may be drawndown.

Fair value: The value at which an asset could be exchanged in an arm's length transaction. Government grants towards the cost of the acquisition will generally be deducted from the asset cost. This is also known as the **fair market value**.

Finance charge: That part of the rental payable under a finance lease which represents a payment in respect of the finance which the lessor has provided for the asset. The finance charges are usually equivalent to the excess of the minimum lease payments over fair value of the asset at the start of the lease.

Finance lease: A lease which confers substantially all of the risks and rewards of ownership to the lessee. Under such leases, the rentals can be construed to be payment for the asset on deferred terms. Typically, the rentals will reimburse the lessor with the full cost of the acquisition of the asset and provide the lessor with additional consideration for the finance which is being provided to the lessee.

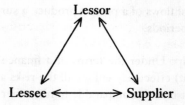

Fixed assets: These are items such as plant and machinery, land and buildings, and vehicles which are used in the business for a number of years.

Fixed charge: This is a security document in respect of a loan and relates to specific assets of a business. It will generally rank in priority to a floating charge. It will not be available to the sole trader or partnership.

Fixed expenses: Costs which do not vary with business activity, e.g. rates.

Floating charge: A floating charge will always be enforceable after a fixed charge, in whichever order they were made, unless it specifically excludes a loan with prior rights on the security of fixed assets and the lender under the fixed charge is aware of this restriction. It will allow the company to deal freely with the assets of the company, but it will not be available to sole traders or partnerships. A floating charge will 'catch' all of the assets of a business upon crystallisation.

Funds flow: Another term for cashflow.

Gearing: The ratio between permanent capital (issued shares and undistributed reserves) and borrowed capital (loans, overdrafts, finance leases, hire purchase, etc.).

General pool of expenditure: The account in which all capital plant and equipment is held for the purposes of computing capital allowances, when those assets are not subject to a short life asset election.

Goodwill: The amount paid for a business over and above the book value of the assets at the date of acquisition. It is an intangible item and as such a valuation will always be subjective and will reflect circumstances at a particular moment in time.

Gross profit: Turnover (sales) less manufacturing costs or the cost of goods sold. Precise definition will vary from industry to industry.

Group relief: The relief for trading losses occurring in companies which are members of a group, which may be offset against the trading profits generated over the same period by other companies which are members of the same group.

Guarantee: Companies may only provide guarantees to the extent they are permitted within the Memorandum of Association. Such powers will usually be found in the objects clause. It will be a contract between three parties, the financier (the creditor), the customer (the principal debtor) and the guarantor (the surety).

Hire purchase (lease purchase): A type of lease under which the lessee has the obligation, or option, to purchase the asset at the end of the term usually for a nominal consideration. The lessee, and not the financier, will generally be able to claim capital allowances in respect of the asset.

IAS 17: The International Accounting Standard on accounting for leases.

Implicit rate of interest: The rate of interest that discounts the minimum lease rentals and the unguaranteed residual value accruing to the lessor to the fair value of the asset.

Inception of a lease: The point at which the lease should first be recorded in financial statements. It will be the earlier of the date the asset is brought into use and the date from which the rentals first accrue.

Indemnity: This is a contract between two parties. These are the indemnifier (the surety) who will contract to make good any loss suffered by the creditor (the financier) as a result of the contract which has been entered into with the debtor (the customer).

Interest cover: This is a measure of the ability of a business to service its existing borrowings out of the profit arising from a single accounting period.

Internal rate of return: A method which finds the discount rate which discounts future cashflows to the same amount as the initial cash outlay.

Keyman insurance: A descriptive term applicable to life only, or life, accident and sickness insurance, which is specifically designed for the business sector.

Landlord's waiver: This is an agreement between the lessee's landlord or debenture holder and the lessor. It is an agreement to ensure that the lessor has the right to remove an asset which could conceivably otherwise be deemed to be afixed to the building.

Letters of comfort: These are documentary evidence from a parent or holding company in respect of a group company. They are rarely enforceable and merely serve for 'moral worth' value as a security document.

Liquid ratio: A measurement of a company's ability to meet its current liabilities from its most readily realisable current assets. It is also known as the acid test.

Master lease: The head agreement which will contain all of the terms and conditions of future leasing contracts. Individual hirings will be controlled by schedules which refer back to the terms and conditions defined in the master lease document, and therefore, the master lease should be signed and dated prior to the first schedule.

Memorandum of satisfaction: This is the instrument used to prove that a charge has been satisfied, following the satisfactory repayment of monies due under the terms of a loan agreement, the security for which was contained in the charge document.

Minimum lease payments: The payments to which the lessee is committed, including all fixed rentals and any guarantee in respect of the residual value.

Net present value: The method which discounts future cashflows back to the start date of the project using a predetermined discount rate. This discounted value is then compared with the initial investment which gave rise to the cashflows.

Ninety per cent test: One of the tests used to compare and contrast a finance lease with an operating lease. The test uses the present value of the minimum lease payments for which the lessee is responsible under the terms of the contract, and compares them to the lessor's net investment in the lease.

Novation agreement: This will often take the form of a simple letter of agreement, drawn up between the financier, the customer and the supplier, in which it is agreed that the financier should be invoiced by the supplier following the delivery of the goods. The financier will only become liable to pay for the goods when the customer is satisfied with them.

Objects clause: This is an express object in the company's Memorandum of Association.

Operating lease: A lease which is not a finance lease. The lessor retains significant risks and rewards of ownership in relation to the leased asset.

Penalty: The description applied to the conditions which apply to contracts under which it is so unfavourable for the customer to cancel (or fail to renew in the case of a lease) that it is reasonable to assume that the customer will not incur that penalty. Generally, leases will be accounted for on such assumptions.

Present value: The value of a future payment or receipt at a point in time given a specified rate of interest. For example, the present value of £110 in one year's time, with interest compounded annually at 10 per cent, is £100.

Primary period: Appertaining principally to leasing, this is the initial period of a finance lease during which the lessor will generally recoup the investment in the leased asset.

Profit margin: A measure of the earning capability of a business. The gross profit margin and the pre-tax profit margins are usually computed.

The **gross profit margin** measures the proportion of overall sales which represents profit to the business, whilst the **pre-tax profit margin** is a measure of the level of profit before tax in every £1 of sales.

Progress payments: Payments which will be required during the construction of a particularly large item of plant and machinery.

Register of charges: The company will be required to keep a register of charges available for public inspection at its registered office.

Regulated agreements: The term used to describe an agreement which falls within the legislation of the Consumer Credit Act 1974. Such agreements arise where the customer is an unincorporated body, such as a partnership or a sole trader, and the balance financed or the total of the lease rentals (including VAT) are £15,000 or less.

Relationship lending: A term used to describe the relationship which subsists between the financier and the established customer. Lines of credit will be marked in anticipation of the development of future business and the financier will remain in close contact with the customer on a regular basis. A close working knowledge of the customer's business will be built up to accommodate future needs swiftly and effectively.

Repurchase agreement: A written undertaking by the supplier of equipment, given to the financier purchasing that equipment, to buy back that equipment at a future date. The agreement may take the form of a put or a call option on behalf of the financier.

Rental rebate: Under the terms of a finance lease, the lessee will generally benefit from the lion's share of the sales proceeds at the end of the lease term. This sum will be treated as a rebate of rentals paid.

Residual value: The value of the leased asset at the end of the lease.

Return on assets: The measurement of the return generated by every £1 of assets held in the business.

Revenue expenses: Items which are properly chargeable against profits in the profit and loss account. These will often include items such as standard software packages, or interest on borrowings to acquire capital, plant and equipment.

Sale and leaseback: An arrangement under which one party sells an asset to another and then enters into a lease of the asset with the purchaser. The seller will warrant that he or she has good title to pass to the purchaser upon completion.

Sales agency: At the end of a finance lease, the customer (lessee) will generally be appointed as the agent of the lessor for the purposes of disposing of the assets which were the subject to the lease. The lessee will then be able to retain the bulk of the sales proceeds, either as a sales agency commission, or as a refund of rentals already paid.

Sales aid: A term used to describe a symbiotic relationship between the dealer (or manufacturer) of capital plant and equipment, and the financier, wherein the dealer's staff will sell the financier's product as a means to overcome the customer's price objections at the point of sale. The dealer will benefit by achieving more sales and the financier will benefit from additional business, thereby increasing the size of the financier's customer base.

Secondary period: The next stage of a finance lease which follows the primary period. The secondary term will often be optional and the rentals will generally be charged at a peppercorn rate.

Share capital: This will be divided into two categories – authorised and issued:

1. Authorised share capital represents the total number of shares which a company may issue in a specific category.
2. Issued share capital represents the value of the shares issued at the time the accounts are drawn up. Shares may be issued:
   (a) at par: meaning the person subscribing for the shares has paid their face value. They will be fully paid up shares.
   (b) as partly paid: in which case the subscriber has only paid a proportion of the face value. The shareholder will be liable to pay up the remaining value when called upon to do so.
   (c) at a premium: where the shares are attractive to their market and the subscriber is willing to pay the market rate which is in excess of the face value. When a company issues its shares at a premium, the excess above their par value will be held in the share premium account.

Short life asset election: The Finance Act of 1985 introduced provisions which allowed for the owner of equipment retained for use in the business to accelerate the capital allowances. This is possible where the equipment is sold, or otherwise disposed of, on or before the fourth anniversary of the end of the year of acquisition. This period is known as the relevant period.

It is necessary to make an election to the Revenue in respect of short life assets within two years of the end of the year of acquisition. If an election is made, the owner of the goods will be able to balance the tax written-down value of the asset against the proceeds arising on sale.

Statement of practice: The manner in which the Inland Revenue gives notice of its policy in considering issues which arise in the assessment of income to taxation. The Statement of Practice will assist in making certain that each office of the Inland Revenue adopts a common approach to the assessment process.

Statements of Practice will be issued from time to time and will deal with all aspects of capital and income taxation.

Statement of standard accounting practice: Published by the Accounting Standards Board, a central body representing the accounting professions, in order to ascertain that company accounts are drawn up on a standard basis. Parties who are interested in the accounts are then able to compare the results on a common basis within an industry.

A Statement is generally preceded by an Exposure Draft, which is a discussion document from which the Accounting Standard will eventually evolve. The Statement is often abbreviated to SSAP.

Stock turnover: A measure of the number of times a company turns over its stock. However, large contracts may distort the figure from one year to another. In general, stock turnover analysis should indicate whether there is some element of obsolete stock in the balance sheet figure when one year is compared with another.

Straight line method: A method of profit recognition from a finance contract. Under this method, the finance charge is divided equally by the number of accounting periods, and a constant amount is then recognised within each period. Because of its simplicity, the method is only likely to be used where the amount of the finance charge is small in relation to the overall size of the accounts in question.

Sub letting agreements: Assets which are subject to a financing agreement may be sublet to another party once the financier has indicated agreement. Generally, the subletting will be formally recognised within an agreement to that effect.

Sum of digits method (rule of 78): A method of apportioning finance charges to accounting periods so as to arrive at an estimation of the results obtained under the actuarial method. It is often easier to calculate using this method, although the result will only be a reasonable approximation, where the finance charge is relatively small in relation to the capital value of the contract.

The formula to express the component of finance charge during any given period is as follows:

$$\frac{n(n + 1)}{2}$$

Where n = the number of periods (months) in the contract. For example in a twelve month contract where $n = 12$:

$$\frac{12(12 + 1)}{2} = 78$$

The unit of finance charge computed in this case using the formula will be 78.

Therefore in month one, where it is assumed that the element of finance charge is at its greatest, 12/78ths of the rental will represent finance charge. During month two, 11/78ths of the rental will represent finance charge. Ultimately, in month twelve (the final month) only 1/78th of the rental will represent finance charge, the remainder being applied to reduce the outstanding capital.

Sustainable growth rate: A measurement which attempts to assess how much growth in turnover has been funded by growth in the business rather than by additional borrowing.

Swap arrangements: A swap arrangement seeks to match the relative strengths of two borrowers and to provide their desired form of finance.

For example, company A is in a position where it can raise fixed rate finance at a favourable rate, whereas company B is able to raise floating rate finance at a favourable rate. If company A has a need for floating rate finance and company B has a need for fixed rate finance, then the two could enter into an interest rate swap.

Following this, company A would have a floating interest rate commitment and company B a fixed rate commitment. The companies would meet their interest obligations, and on maturity of the loans they would be primarily responsible for the funds which they had initially raised (company A for the fixed rate loan and company B for the floating interest rate loan). Any difference in the financing costs between the fixed and the floating rate arrangements are termed the 'swap payments'.

Tax-based funding: A term used to describe facilities wherein the customer payments are computed to reflect tax benefits available to the financier, who is also the owner of the equipment. Lease, operating lease and contract hire facilities fall into this category.

Non-tax-based financing implies that there will be no tax allowances to reflect in the repayment cashflows.

Tax delays: A reference to the period of time after the end of a company's accounting period before which tax will fall due and payable (or a refund will be receivable).

Tax variation clause: A clause within a lease contract which allows the lessor to vary the amount and timing of rentals during the term of the lease in order to reflect changes in the actual tax benefits which were assumed in the lease pricing.

Tax shelter: A descriptive term indicating the financier's ability to utilise tax allowances available as a result of the purchase of capital plant and equipment, or vehicles. There will be sufficient profits, subject to tax, from which those allowances may be deducted.

Term: The period of a financial contract, which for accounting purposes, is deemed to include any extension due to bargains or penalties.

Trading: The lessor will need to become established as carrying on the trade of leasing in order to be able to claim and retain the capital allowances. If the lessor's business is structured in such a way as to imply that it is simply dealing in capital goods, it will be in danger of losing its right to allowances. The trade of leasing must therefore be seen to be active.

Tax written down value: The value of an asset in the owner's books of account after deduction (from the cost price) of the capital allowances which have been claimed.

Unincorporated business: A business the liabilities of which are not limited by the issue of shares – a business which is neither a limited company, nor a plc. The owners of an unincorporated business will generally have unlimited personal responsibility for the liabilities of their business.

Unregulated agreements: These are agreements which are outside the scope of the Consumer Credit Act 1974.

Variable expenses: Costs which are activity related, i.e. they vary in amount with the level of activity. Examples are vehicle operating costs such as fuel, repair or maintenance.

Working capital ratio: This is also known as the current asset ratio. It is a measure of a company's liquidity.

INDEX